"Danny Akin consis [obscured] cholarly rigor, pastoral insight, and [obscured] nly educate you; they move you. These insights come from a lifetime of studying Scripture, communion with the Spirit, and walking humbly with God as a husband, father, and leader."

J. D. Greear, pastor, The Summit Church, Raleigh-Durham, NC

"It should go without saying that the longest chapter in the Bible deserves a strong reverential study. This is especially true as it is the most in-depth revelation of the power and authority of the Bible in the Bible. Put simply, Danny Akin gives this psalm the study that it deserves and much more. You will be blessed and encouraged as you are reminded in this study why this book called the Bible stands above all other books. I highly commend it and recommend it."

James Merritt, pastor of Cross Pointe Church, host of Touching Lives, former president of the Southern Baptist Convention

"Danny Akin loves to teach and preach the Word of God, and he is at his very best as he teaches the majestic 119th Psalm. This is a treasure of biblical truth, and it will help every Christian to grow into greater love for the Word of God and for the great and gracious God who has given us his Word. This book is a devotional treasure and a faithful commentary combined into one powerful book."

R. Albert Mohler Jr., president, The Southern Baptist Theological Seminary

"It gives me great pleasure to recommend Exalting Jesus in Psalm 119 by Daniel Akin as part of the Christ-Centered Exposition Commentary series. Psalm 119, the longest of the biblical psalms, is longer than thirty of the sixty-six books of the entire Bible. The psalm is composed of twenty-two sections (eight verses in each section) corresponding to the twenty-two letters of the Hebrew alphabet. Akin examines every verse of each section, presents the main idea of each section, and concludes with ten thought-provoking questions that present challenges for readers to cherish and to obey God's Word. The analysis exhibits an excellent model for expository preaching while never departing from a focus on the value of treasuring and meditating on God's Word. Psalm 119 is truly the Mount Everest of the biblical psalms, an expanded treatment of the blessed man of Psalm 1. Allow Akin to guide you and help you reflect on this psalm, which is an infallible guide for conduct and an unspeakable source of comfort."

Mark Rooker, senior professor of Old Testament and Hebrew, Southeastern Baptist Theological Seminary

CHRIST-CENTERED

Exposition

OT / COMMENTARY

AUTHOR Daniel L. Akin

SERIES EDITORS David Platt, Daniel L. Akin, and Tony Merida

CHRIST-CENTERED

Exposition

EXALTING JESUS IN

PSALM 119

BRENTWOOD, TENNESSEE

B&H Publishing Group
Brentwood, Tennessee

ISBN: 978-1-0877-2449-2

Dewey Decimal Classification: 220.7
Subject Heading: BIBLE. O.T. PSALMS—
COMMENTARIES\JESUS CHRIST

Printed in the United States of America
3 4 5 6 7 8 9 10 • 27 26 25 24 23

SERIES DEDICATION

Dedicated to Adrian Rogers and John Piper. They have taught us to love the gospel of Jesus Christ, to preach the Bible as the inerrant Word of God, to pastor the church for which our Savior died, and to have a passion to see all nations gladly worship the Lamb.

—David Platt, Tony Merida, and Danny Akin
March 2013

AUTHOR'S DEDICATION

I delight in dedicating this volume to my four sons, Nate, Jon, Paul, and Tim. Your love for the Word of God is so evident in your lives and ministries. You make your dad proud.

TABLE OF CONTENTS

ACKNOWLEDGMENTS

Thank you, Devin Moncada, Kim Humphrey, and Kimberly Rochelle, for your invaluable assistance in producing this volume. Each of you is a personal gift from God to me.

SERIES INTRODUCTION

Augustine said, "Where Scripture speaks, God speaks." The editors of the Christ-Centered Exposition Commentary series believe that where God speaks, the pastor must speak. God speaks through His written Word. We must speak from that Word. We believe the Bible is God breathed, authoritative, inerrant, sufficient, understandable, necessary, and timeless. We also affirm that the Bible is a Christ-centered book; that is, it contains a unified story of redemptive history of which Jesus is the hero. Because of this Christ-centered trajectory that runs from Genesis 1 through Revelation 22, we believe the Bible has a corresponding global-missions thrust. From beginning to end, we see God's mission as one of making worshipers of Christ from every tribe and tongue worked out through this redemptive drama in Scripture. To that end we must preach the Word.

In addition to these distinct convictions, the Christ-Centered Exposition Commentary series has some distinguishing characteristics. First, this series seeks to display exegetical accuracy. What the Bible says is what we want to say. While not every volume in the series will be a verse-by-verse commentary, we nevertheless desire to handle the text carefully and explain it rightly. Those who teach and preach bear the heavy responsibility of saying what God has said in His Word and declaring what God has done in Christ. We desire to handle God's Word faithfully, knowing that we must give an account for how we have fulfilled this holy calling (Jas 3:1).

Second, the Christ-Centered Exposition Commentary series has pastors in view. While we hope others will read this series, such as parents, teachers, small-group leaders, and student ministers, we desire to provide a commentary busy pastors will use for weekly preparation of biblically faithful and gospel-saturated sermons. This series is not academic in nature. Our aim is to present a readable and pastoral style of commentaries. We believe this aim will serve the church of the Lord Jesus Christ.

Third, we want the Christ-Centered Exposition Commentary series to be known for the inclusion of helpful illustrations and theologically driven applications. Many commentaries offer no help in illustrations, and few offer any kind of help in application. Often those that do offer illustrative material and application unfortunately give little serious attention to the text. While giving ourselves primarily to explanation, we also hope to serve readers by providing inspiring and illuminating illustrations coupled with timely and timeless application.

Finally, as the name suggests, the editors seek to exalt Jesus from every book of the Bible. In saying this, we are not commending wild allegory or fanciful typology. We certainly believe we must be constrained to the meaning intended by the divine Author himself, the Holy Spirit of God. However, we also believe the Bible has a messianic focus, and our hope is that the individual authors will exalt Christ from particular texts. Luke 24:25-27,44-47 and John 5:39,46 inform both our hermeneutics and our homiletics. Not every author will do this the same way or have the same degree of Christ-centered emphasis. That is fine with us. We believe faithful exposition that is Christ centered is not monolithic. We do believe, however, that we must read the whole Bible as Christian Scripture. Therefore, our aim is both to honor the historical particularity of each biblical passage and to highlight its intrinsic connection to the Redeemer.

The editors are indebted to the contributors of each volume. The reader will detect a unique style from each writer, and we celebrate these unique gifts and traits. While distinctive in their approaches, the authors share a common characteristic in that they are pastoral theologians. They love the church, and they regularly preach and teach God's Word to God's people. Further, many of these contributors are younger voices. We think these new, fresh voices can serve the church well, especially among a rising generation that has the task of proclaiming the Word of Christ and the Christ of the Word to the lost world.

We hope and pray this series will serve the body of Christ well in these ways until our Savior returns in glory. If it does, we will have succeeded in our assignment.

David Platt
Daniel L. Akin
Tony Merida
Series Editors
February 2013

Psalm 119

How to Be Blessed and Blameless before the Lord

PSALM 119:1-8

Main Idea: A blessed and blameless life comes by keeping, treasuring, and meditating on the Lord's Word.

I. **Walk according to the Lord's Instruction (119:1).**
II. **Seek the Lord with All Your Heart (119:2).**
III. **Walk in the Lord's Ways (119:3).**
IV. **Diligently Keep the Lord's Precepts (119:4).**
V. **Commit Your Ways to the Lord's Statutes (119:5).**
VI. **Meditate on the Lord's Commands (119:6).**
VII. **Learn about the Lord's Righteous Judgments (119:7).**
VIII. **Keep the Lord's Statutes (119:8).**

In his treatise "On Christian Freedom" (1520), the reformer Martin Luther (1483–1546) wrote concerning the Bible,

> One thing and one only is necessary for Christian life, righteousness and liberty. That one thing is the most holy Word of God, the Gospel of Christ. . . . Let us then consider it certain and conclusively established that the soul can do without all things except the Word of God, and that where this is not there is no help for the soul in anything else whatever. But if it has the Word it is rich and lacks nothing, since this Word is the Word of Life, of truth, of light, of peace, of righteousness, of salvation, of joy, of liberty, of wisdom, of power, of grace, of glory and of every blessing beyond our power to estimate. This is why the prophet in the entire Psalm [119], and in many other places of Scripture with so many sighs yearns after the Word of God. (Luther, *The Christian in Society*, 314)

Luther's words beautifully describe Psalm 119, one of the most important, valuable, and precious texts in all Scripture. It is the "Word of God" psalm with so many unique features:

It is the longest chapter in the Bible with 176 verses. It is longer than seventeen books in the New Testament and longer than each of the Minor Prophets with the exceptions of Hosea and Zechariah.

It is an alphabetic acrostic psalm, like Lamentations 3, built on the twenty-two letters of the Hebrew alphabet. Each verse in each stanza begins with the same letter. For example, each of the first eight verses begins with the letter *Aleph* (א) in Hebrew. If this had been composed in English, verses 1-8 each would begin with the letter *A*.

Almost every verse makes reference to the Word of God. Franz Delitzsch well says of Psalm 119 that it is

> "the Christian's golden A B C of the praise, love, power and use of the word of God"; for here we have set forth in inexhaustible fullness what the word of God is to a man, and how a man is to behave himself in relation to it. (Keil and Delitzsch, *Psalms*, 735–36)

At least eight different terms or synonyms are used in reference to the Word of God: "instruction" or "law" (*torah*) twenty-five times; "word" (*dabar*) twenty-four times; "judgments" or "ordinances" (*mispatim*) twenty-three times; "decrees" (*hedot*) twenty-three times; "commands" (*mitswoth*) twenty-two times; "statutes" (*chuqqim*) twenty-one times; "precepts" (*piqqudim*) twenty-one times; "promise" or "word" (*'imra*) nineteen times (Boice, *Psalms 107–150*, 971).

Stanza one, stanza *Aleph*, gives eight truths that lead to a blessed and blameless life before the Lord.

Walk according to the Lord's Instructions

PSALM 119:1

Psalm 119 is composed of various genres: law, lament, praise, innocence, confidence, and celebration. However, it is "best to call it a wisdom psalm" (Ross, *Psalms,* 461; cf. VanGemeren, *Psalms,* 858). Verse 1 echoes Psalm 1, another wisdom psalm. It is a twofold blessing for those who walk in the Word. Happy, fortunate, and blessed are those persons "whose way is blameless" and "who walk according to the LORD's instruction." It is easy to see how the two ideas support each other.

Blameless people are people of integrity (cf. Ps 101; 1 Tim 3:1). Their manner of life is above reproach. They conduct themselves wisely because they walk in the Word. Like the man of Psalm 1, such a person "delight[s] is in the Lord's instruction, and he meditates on it day and night" (Ps 1:2). This man is blessed because he is blameless. His life knows nothing of duplicity or hypocrisy. There is no pretense in this man. He rejoices that happiness and holiness are his wonderful companions.

Seek the Lord with All Your Heart

PSALM 119:2

Verse 2 has a second blessing, and it may be the key that unlocks the entire psalm. The blessed person seeks the Lord "with all his heart." This person passionately pursues his Lord above all else. And he understands that knowledge of God is discovered in his Word, "his decrees." The word translated "decrees" or "testimonies" has covenantal connotations. Spurgeon says,

> Blessedness is ascribed to those who treasure up the testimonies of the Lord: in which is implied that they search the Scriptures, that they come to an understanding of them, that they love them, and then that they continue in practice of them. We must first get a thing before we can keep it. (*Treasury*, 141)

Jeremiah 29:13 reminds us, "You will seek me and find me when you search for me with all your heart." Keep his decrees. Seek him with your whole heart. Be blessed!

Walk in the Lord's Ways

PSALM 119:3

This verse echoes the wisdom of verse 1 and flows naturally from verse 2. If we seek the Lord with all our heart, we will not practice wrongdoing. *The Message* paraphrases, "You don't go off on your own." Staying close to the Lord, we will "walk in his ways." God's Word is our compass. His Word guides our course of conduct, our daily walk. God's Word maps out our life. It forms our habits and directs our pursuits. Ligon Duncan says, "The way of the Lord is about walk, not talk" ("Not by Bread Alone"). He is right. People like that do not merely say the right things; they do the right things. Out of what I call gospel gratitude, they live out the word of the gospel of Jesus Christ that has transformed them and made them a new creation (2 Cor 5:17).

Diligently Keep the Lord's Precepts

PSALM 119:4

God's Word does not have suggestions for our consideration. They are commands from a king who demands our obedience. God's "precepts," his instructions, come to us with the force of a command, a divine order. They are God's ("your") precepts. Derek Kidner says, "The word points to the particular instructions of the Lord, as one who cares about detail" (*Psalms,* 418). And because these are the sovereign Lord's particular instructions, they are to be "diligently kept." We are to obey God's Word fully and completely. Partial obedience is complete disobedience, just as partial faithfulness or honesty is complete unfaithfulness and dishonesty. We must delightfully fixate on keeping the instructions of our Lord. They are not a burden. They are our joy.

Commit Your Ways to the Lord's Statutes

PSALM 119:5

Verses 5-8 shift to a first-person perspective. The psalmist expresses, in a deeply personal way, his desire to obey the teachings of the Bible. Six personal pronouns fill these last four verses. The blessed man says to the Lord, "If only my ways were committed to keeping your statutes." This is the third time he uses the word "ways" (vv. 1,3). The psalmist prays that his ways will line up with God's ways. Further, he wants to be "committed" (meaning diligent, disciplined, and consistent) in keeping and obeying the Lord's statutes. Ross notes, "The word for 'statutes' here and in verse 8 emphasizes the binding nature of God's law. By keeping these statutes, one's conduct will be steadfast" (*Psalms,* 470). The psalmist is aware that our human hearts are prone to wander. He knows we do not naturally keep God's statutes. He readily acknowledges his need for God to enable him to be steadfast in his obedience.

Meditate on the Lord's Commands

PSALM 119:6

Steadfast obedience has a wonderful and blessed result: "Then I would not be ashamed." Christians cannot lose their salvation. However, we can be put to shame. Our failure to obey the will of our heavenly Father can embarrass us. Spurgeon well says, "Sin brings shame, and when sin is gone, the reason for being ashamed is banished" (*Treasury*, 144). Adam and Eve had no experience of shame until they listened to Satan and disobeyed the Lord (Gen 3). The same is true for us. To whose voice will we listen? The psalmist has the answer: "I think about all your commands." The ESV says the psalmist's eyes are "fixed" on God's commandments, which means to gaze at with intensity, to pay attention to carefully, and to dwell on and meditate. The psalmist says he will glue his eyes on all God's commands in order not to be put to shame. In other words, he says, "I will not pick and choose the parts of the Word that I will obey. All of your Word, for all of me, all of the time will be my ambition and holy pursuit. There will be no part-time Christianity for me."

Learn about the Lord's Righteous Judgments

PSALM 119:7

Verse 2 instructed us to seek the Lord with our whole heart. Now in verse 7 we declare that we will praise the Lord with an "upright heart." Praise flows naturally from an upright heart that has fixed its eyes on all the commands of the Lord (v. 6) and that has learned his righteous rules, his righteous decisions (v. 7). Obedience is not a burden. It is not a life of dullness and drudgery. It is a life of delight, praise, joy, and blessedness. Learning the Word of God, his ways and wisdom, is a call to discipleship. It is a call to be a diligent student of the Word. To love God, we must know God. Bible study leads to praise. Theology leads to praise. Spurgeon beautifully says, "We must learn to praise, learn that we may praise, and praise when we have learned" (*Treasury*, 145). The Bible is a songbook, a music book. Study it and you will soon find yourself singing about it and about the Savior to whom it points.

Keep the Lord's Statutes

PSALM 119:8

This first stanza ends on a note of resolve: "I will keep your statutes" (cf. v. 5). The psalmist resolves with his whole heart (v. 2) and an "upright heart" (v. 7) to obey God's Word—"all your commands" (cf. v. 6). This is not a boastful declaration since he gives a humble and heartfelt request: "never abandon me" (cf. Ps 22:1).

The psalmist was in some difficulty or distress. This should not surprise us. Second Timothy 3:12 reminds us, "All who want to live a godly life in Christ Jesus will be persecuted." The psalmist understands that our striving after obedience is worthless without the presence of our Lord. Feelings will certainly ebb and flow. However, in his Word we have a sure and certain promise, "I will never leave you or abandon you" (Heb 13:5). With such a promise we can press on. With such a promise, we can continually praise the Lord.

Conclusion

Psalm 119 is not only a beautiful portrait of the perfect *written* Word of God but also a beautiful portrait of the perfect *living* Word of God. Jesus alone is the truly blameless man who walks in the Word and seeks his Lord with his whole heart. Walking in the ways of his Father, he did no wrong and diligently kept the precepts, statutes, and commands of Holy Scripture. And when he died on the cross for the sins of the world (John 1:29), although abandoned while the wrath of God was poured out on him as our penal substitute (Ps 22:1), he was not utterly and forever abandoned. He prayed with his final breath, "Father, into your hands I entrust my spirit" (Luke 23:46). Jesus of Nazareth is the Psalm 119 man. In a true and real sense, "every line speaks of Jesus" (Reardon, *Christ in the Psalms*, 238).

Reflect and Discuss

1. What does it mean to be blessed? How does the Bible's conception of blessing differ from the world's?
2. What are this psalm's criteria for knowing whether you are seeking the Lord with your whole heart? Are any of these missing from your life currently?
3. How can the promise of Jeremiah 29:13 encourage you when it is difficult to want to seek God? How can you rely on other believers to help you?
4. Why is obedience intimately connected to God's Word in Psalm 119?
5. This stanza teaches that partial obedience is complete disobedience, just as partial faithfulness or honesty is complete unfaithfulness and dishonesty. What does partial obedience and faithfulness look like compared to complete obedience and faithfulness?
6. Why should you be concerned with obeying God's Word?

7. In what way is one's praise connected to one's heart? What does this teach you about the remedy for when you or someone else does not praise God?
8. What is something you have learned about God in Scripture that immediately led you to praise him? Why do you think that happened?
9. In what place in your life can you resolve to obey God's Word more diligently?
10. In what ways do you see Jesus living out this first part of Psalm 119 in the Gospels?

How Can We Live a Life of Purity?

PSALM 119:9-16

Main Idea: Prioritize God's Word in your life, affections, and thoughts so that you live a holy and pure life.

I. Guard the Word of God in Your Life (119:9).
II. Seek the Lord with All Your Heart (119:10).
III. Treasure the Word of God in Your Heart (119:11).
IV. Let the Lord Teach You His Statutes (119:12).
V. Proclaim the Lord's Wisdom with Your Words (119:13).
VI. Rejoice in the Lord's Decrees (119:14).
VII. Meditate on the Lord's Precepts (119:15).
VIII. Delight in the Lord's Statutes (119:16).
IX. Do Not Forget the Word of God (119:16).

One of my heroes in the gospel ministry is Adrian Rogers (1931–2005). He pastored the historic Bellevue Baptist Church in Memphis from 1972 to 2005 and served as president of the SBC three times (1979–1980; 1986–1988). He led Southern Baptists to reaffirm, without apology, the inerrancy, infallibility, and sufficiency of the Bible. During what is now known as the Conservative Resurgence, Rogers was asked to serve on what became known as the Peace Committee. Rogers and the other committee members were responsible for reaching a compromise between liberal and conservative Baptists on theological doctrines, especially the doctrine of the Bible's inspiration. At one point in their meetings, a lawyer who represented the moderate or liberal perspective approached Rogers. During this conversation Rogers made a famous statement that defined the heart of the controversy. The lawyer pulled Rogers aside and said, "Adrian, if you don't compromise, we will never get together" (quoted in Akin and Curtis, "Adrian Rogers," 485–86). Rogers's reply was simple and direct:

> I'm willing to compromise about many things, but not the Word of God. So far as getting together is concerned, we don't have to get together. The Southern Baptist Convention, as it is, does not have to survive. I don't have to be the pastor of Bellevue Baptist Church. I don't have to be loved; I don't

even have to live. But I will not compromise the Word of God. (Joyce Rogers, *Love Worth Finding*, 109–10)

Why was Adrian Rogers so passionate about the Bible? Why was he so unwilling to compromise on the Word of God? There are many reasons, but one appears in Psalm 119:11: "I have treasured your word in my heart so that I may not sin against you." Rogers knew what the evangelist D. L. Moody knew: "This book will keep you from sin, or sin will keep you from this book."[1]

Psalm 119:9-16 is the second stanza of this acrostic psalm patterned after the twenty-two letters of the Hebrew alphabet. Since *Beth* (ב) is the second letter, each line in this stanza starts with a word that begins with the Hebrew letter *Beth*. The stanza also begins with a perennial question that is especially relevant in our current American context: "How can a young man [and for that matter, an old man!] keep his way pure?" With the issues of sexual assault, abuse, and harassment dominating the media and the culture, what can the man of God, the devoted follower of Jesus Christ, do to live a life of unquestionable moral purity? Psalm 119 clearly answers that our relationship to the Word of God determines whether we will live holy lives. Stanza *Beth* gives nine admonitions for our careful reflection and meditation concerning our relationship to Scripture. They provide a divinely inspired road map to a pure and holy life.

Guard the Word of God in Your Life

PSALM 119:9

Verse 9 begins with a rhetorical question every Christian, especially a young one, struggles with, How can I live a pure and holy life that is pleasing to my Lord? Verses 9-16 provide the answer. The first action is defensive: "By keeping your word." We guard or protect the Word of God in our life. As a result, the Word of God performs guard duty and acts as a sentinel that keeps us from sin. When we keep the Word in a safe place in our lives, the Word protects us and keeps us safe from impurity in both thought and action. As we guard our life by the Word of God, the Word of God guards us.

In John 17:17 Jesus prayed this prayer for us: "Sanctify them by the truth; your word is truth." He then adds in verse 19, "I sanctify myself

---

[1] Many know Moody for this quote, but it is also said to be written in the cover of the Bible of John Bunyan, the author of *Pilgrim's Progress*.

for them, so that they also may be sanctified by the truth." Jesus kept the Word in a safe place in his life as he made his way to the cross. "Blameless" (Ps 119:1) and with an "upright heart" (v. 7), the pure, spotless, and sinless Son of God guarded the Word as it guided him to Calvary. He sets a perfect example for us to follow.

Seek the Lord with All Your Heart

PSALM 119:10

Verses 10-11 are the most crucial to living a holy and pure life because they focus on the heart, the inner man, the real you on the inside. Because we guard our way by the Word in verse 9, we strive to seek the giver of the Word in verse 10. And our seeking is not half-hearted! "I have sought you with all my heart." The ESV has "with my whole heart." We guard our ways by having the Lord's Word in our life. With diligence, passion, and sincerity, we must seek our Lord.

Suddenly the psalmist makes a short prayer of petition: "Don't let me wander from your commands." There is much wisdom in this request. Proverbs 19:27 reminds us, "If you stop listening to correction, my son, you will stray from the words of knowledge." The psalmist knew that it is easier to make a promise to God than to keep it. He seeks the Lord with his whole heart, but he recognizes that he needs God's help to succeed. Charles Spurgeon says it well:

> The man of God exerts himself, but does not trust himself. . . . He knows that even his whole strength is not enough to keep him right unless his King shall be his keeper, and he who made the commands shall make him constant in obeying them. (*Treasury*, 158)

It is hard to wander from the Lord's commands when you seek him with your whole heart.

Treasure the Word of God in Your Heart

PSALM 119:11

Verse 11 is one of the most well known in all the Bible. Many people memorized it as a child in Vacation Bible School. The KJV is still the most familiar, "Thy word have I hid in mine heart, that I might not sin against thee." However, the CSB captures the original intent of the psalmist a bit better: "I have treasured your word in my heart so that I may not sin against you." The Word of God "is so valuable it will be preserved in the heart (that is, the mind) for any appropriate use. . . . The word will be continually at his disposal to determine his actions" (Ross, *Psalms,* 477). John Piper provides additional insight with his thoughts on the importance of the heart:

> Take the phrase "in my heart." The point here is mainly to say: inside of me, not just on a tablet outside of me. The words of God are not just kept in writing for the psalmist to consult outside of himself. They are kept for his consulting inside of him—in his heart. The heart of the Old Testament is a place of both thinking and feeling (Genesis 6:5; Job 36:13). So these words of God are being treasured in a place where they can be thought about and felt. ("Thy Word I Have Treasured in My Heart")

We would be negligent in applying this verse if we did not at least note the value of Scripture memorization. Dallas Willard provides a wise perspective when he writes,

> As a pastor, teacher, and counselor I have repeatedly seen the transformation of inner and outer life that comes simply from memorization and meditation upon Scripture. Personally, I would never undertake to pastor a church or guide a program of Christian education that did not involve a continuous program of memorization of the choicest passages of Scripture for people of all ages. (*The Spirit of the Disciplines,* 150)

The psalmist knew that the key to a pure life is a pure heart made clean by the Word of God. Paul knew this too and provides words of wisdom to his young son in the ministry. Second Timothy 2:22 is a beautiful complement to verse 11: "Flee from youthful passions, and pursue righteousness, faith, love, and peace, along with those who call on the Lord from a pure heart." A pure heart will mean a pure life.

Let the Lord Teach You His Statutes

PSALM 119:12

Verse 12 is a simple prayer of two parts. First, there is praise; then there is a petition. The praise is, "LORD, may you be blessed." The songwriter praises God, adores him, and thanks him for his Word. In that light he says, "Teach me your statutes." He wants the Lord to help him be faithful and "loyal to the terms of the covenant" between the Lord and his people (VanGemeren, *Psalms*, 850). VanGemeren points out that "the teachable spirit begins with proper regard for God" (ibid., 862). The psalmist praises the Lord. Now he wants the Lord to teach him more of his Word, his instruction, his commands.

Verse 12 is nothing less than an Old Testament call to discipleship. It finds a New Testament echo in the Great Commission of Matthew 28:19-20. Making disciples of all nations means that we teach them everything the risen Lord Jesus has commanded. All of his statutes are for all of his people. The Bible clearly commends godly and gifted teachers for our benefit and edification. However, verse 12 reminds us there is a better Teacher still.

Proclaim the Lord's Wisdom with Your Words

PSALM 119:13

In verse 12 we were taught the Word. Now in verse 13 we "declare" (ESV) and "proclaim" (CSB) the Word! For all our life, we must verbally "recite aloud" (NLT) all that we hear from the Lord's mouth. From his mouth to our mouths, the Word of God must resound throughout our lives. We must not neglect any of it. We must proclaim it "all."

Take note that the judgments, the rules, the regulations we declare are words that come from the "mouth" of God. This verse teaches a theological truth by means of an anthropomorphism. Paul could have had this phrase in mind when he wrote in 2 Timothy 3:16, "All Scripture is inspired by God." Here the doctrine of the Bible's inspiration ascends to the highest level. The logic is clear. A perfect God will only speak perfect words. Thus Thomas Manton (1620–1677), the English Puritan and chaplain to Oliver Cromwell, says,

> That which should be declared and taught in the church should not be our own opinions and fancies, but the pure word of God; not the vanity of our thoughts, but the verity of his revelations. (*Psalm 119*, vol. 1, 109)

Rejoice in the Lord's Decrees

PSALM 119:14

Verse 14 rings with the sound of celebration as the psalmist reflects on the value of God's Word. It recalls Psalm 1:2 and anticipates what we will find later in this psalm.

Instruction from your lips is better for me than thousands of gold and silver pieces. (Ps 119:72)

Since I love your commands more than gold, even the purest gold. (Ps 119:127)

The one who allows the Lord to be his Teacher (v. 12) rejoices in the revelation of God's decrees. How much does he rejoice? He declares, "As much as in all riches." In other words, he cannot put a price tag on how valuable God's Word is to him. Even if he were to collect all the riches in the world, they would pale in comparison. He would not trade God's Word for anything this world has to offer. His treasure is God, not gold. His treasure is God's eternal Word, not temporal wealth.

A man will treasure what he delights in (v. 11). A man will also proclaim and speak of that which he delights (v. 13). For the psalmist, it is the Lord (v. 10) and his Word (v. 14). What is it for you and me?

Meditate on the Lord's Precepts

PSALM 119:15

Verse 15 draws attention to the spiritual discipline of meditation and again recalls Psalm 1:2, where we read that the righteous meditate on God's Word "day and night." The psalmist declares that he will "meditate" on the Lord's "precepts" and that he will "think about ["fix my eyes on" ESV] your ways." There is an important connection to verse 9 and the way of the psalmist. If followers of Jesus meditate and think about God's ways, then his ways will become their ways. And because his way is pure, their way will be pure.

Meditating on God's Word is a lost art in our day that we desperately need to recover. Ross points out that meditation has the idea of "a thoughtful concentration on God's word," but it is not limited to that (*Psalms*, 479). He notes it may also include "musing, talking, or even singing to oneself" God's Word (ibid.). Spurgeon's thoughts here are helpful:

> He who has an inward delight in anything will not long withdraw his mind from it. As a miser often returns to look upon his treasure, so does the devout believer by frequent meditation turn over the priceless wealth which he has discovered in the book of the Lord. To some men meditation is a task; to the man of cleansed way it is a joy. (*Treasury*, 161)

Delight in the Lord's Statutes

PSALM 119:16

In verse 12 we pray, asking the Lord to "teach" us his statutes. Now in verse 16 we declare, "I will delight in your statutes." What we ask for, we receive. God teaches us. And what we receive, we delight in! We delight in his Word, here called his "statutes." James Boice says the word "delight" in verse 16 carries the idea of "a settled pleasure" (*Psalms 107–150*, 981). Delight has followed meditation, which followed treasuring God's Word more than all riches. God's Word to the songwriter is a blessing, not a burden. It is his drink, his food, his life. It is his happiness and joy. Adam Clarke said of his delight in God's Word, "I will skip about and jump for joy" (in Spurgeon, *Treasury*, 170).

Do Not Forget the Word of God

PSALM 119:16

Because God's Word is his delight, the songwriter says, "I will not forget" it. After all, "Love for God's word is love for God" (VanGemeren, *Psalms*, 863). To honor and fulfill this pledge, there are seven daily, practical applications of this text:

- Carry a Bible, electronically or as a book, with you.
- Read your Bible.
- Study your Bible.
- Meditate on your Bible.
- Love your Bible.
- Share your Bible.
- Thank God for your Bible.

Ross summarizes the psalm so very well:

> This "*Bet* Stanza" has to do with keeping our lives pure by avoiding sin, which is done by knowing the word of God so well that it is always on our minds to correct and to guide us through life. But this is no fixed duty; for the believer the word is like a treasure, more delightful and useful than riches. The LORD is the teacher, his word and his way the lesson, and righteousness the result. (*Psalms*, 480)

Conclusion

Inside many of the New Testaments distributed by the wonderful Christian organization known as the Gideons, you will also find these sentences:

> The Bible contains the mind of God, the state of man, the way of salvation, the doom of sinners, and the happiness of believers. Its doctrines are holy, its precepts are binding, its histories are true, and its decisions are immutable.
>
> Read it to be wise, believe it to be safe, and practice it to be holy. It contains light to direct you, food to support you, and comfort to cheer you.
>
> It is the traveler's map, the pilgrim's staff, the pilot's compass, the soldier's sword, and the Christian's charter. Here Paradise is restored, Heaven is opened, and the gates of Hell disclosed.
>
> Christ is its grand subject, our good the design, and the glory of God its end. It should fill the memory, rule the heart, and guide the feet. Read it slowly, frequently, and prayerfully. It is a mine of wealth, a paradise of glory, and a river of pleasure.
>
> It is given you in life, will be opened at the judgment, and be remembered forever. It involves the highest responsibility, will reward the greatest labor, and will condemn all who trifle with its sacred contents.

Although God did not inspire those words as he did the Bible, they are inspiring. They beautifully capture the treasure that dwells in us when we allow the Word of God to make itself at home in our hearts. Treasure the Word of God in your heart that you might not sin against your God.

Reflect and Discuss

1. Are you concerned with living a holy and pure life? How does this psalm shape what you should be concerned about?
2. In what ways does Scripture guard your life beyond telling you what you ought not to do? How is Scripture more than a book of rules?
3. Can someone say that they have a relationship with the Lord or are seeking the Lord if they do not keep his commands? Why or why not?

4. What role does Scripture memorization currently have in your spiritual life? What benefits have you seen come from this practice? How might you begin to practice memorization in your life more?
5. How can your prayers help you know whether you have a "teachable spirit"? What does a "teachable spirit" pray for?
6. What does it mean to proclaim the Word? What are the different ways you can proclaim the Word in your networks (e.g., home, work, friendships)?
7. If someone were to examine what you talked about this past week, would they know that you delighted in the Lord and his Word? How can you practice expressing your delight in God?
8. How does this stanza's teaching about meditation differ from popular ideas about meditation in our culture?
9. This stanza teaches that God's Word provides joy. Does this mean Christians will feel joyful every time they read Scripture? Why or why not?
10. What are some practical things you can do to help you not forget the Word?

The Wondrous Word of God

PSALM 119:17-24

Main Idea: Resolve to obey the wonderful Word of God because it leads to life.

I. Ask God to Help You Keep His Word (119:17-18).
  A. His Word is life for God's servant (119:17).
  B. His Word is wondrous to God's servant (119:18).

II. Ask God to Help You Stay Faithful in a World That Is Not Your Home (119:19-20).
  A. Know who you are: a person headed to a different kingdom (119:19).
  B. Know what you need: a passion for the Word (119:20).

III. Ask God to Help You When Others Oppose You (119:21-24).
  A. Trust that God will deal with the arrogant and disobedient (119:21).
  A. Trust that God will hear your prayers for relief from persecution (119:22-24).
    1. While you trust him, keep his testimonies (119:22).
    2. While you trust him, meditate on his statutes (119:23).
    3. While you trust him, delight in his counsel (119:24).

The Scriptures teem with marvels; the Bible is a wonder-land. . . . It is itself a world of wonders" (Spurgeon, *Treasury*, 172). These are the words of Charles Spurgeon as he reflected on the third stanza—stanza *Gimel* (ג) (vv. 17-24)—in the "Word of God Psalm," Psalm 119.

These verses seem to be "particularly autobiographical" (Boice, *Psalms 107–150*, 983). Our author is experiencing opposition and persecution for his faith. These words find an echo in the Beatitudes portion of the Sermon on the Mount where our Lord pronounces a blessing on those who are persecuted because of righteousness (Matt 5:10-12). With the psalm's theme of the "servant" (vv. 17,23; cf. Isa 53), it is easy to imagine the Lord Jesus praying this psalm in the garden of Gethsemane on the night he was betrayed and arrested. The Word of God sustained our Savior in his darkest hour. The Word of God will do the same for us.

In difficulty and distress, the Lord and his wondrous Word are both our comforter and our counselor.

Ask God to Help You Keep His Word

PSALM 119:17-18

The stanza easily divides into three movements: verses 17-18, verses 19-20, and verses 21-24. The first movement reminds us of the necessity of obeying God's Word. Jesus said in John 14:15, "If you love me, you will keep my commands." Obedience to the commands of our Lord tangibly and visibly expresses our love for him in our hearts. We gladly and joyfully obey him because we *want* to obey, not because we *have* to obey. Blessings supernaturally flood our lives because we are keeping and obeying God's Word. We see two of them in verses 17-18.

His Word Is Life for God's Servant (119:17)

The psalmist prays and asks that the Lord would "deal generously with your servant." It is a strong and urgent request. In Psalms the phrase "deal generously" carries the idea of deliverance (13:6; 116:7; 142:7) (Ross, *Psalms*, 483). The idea is, "Help me and rescue me."

Who is the one making this request? The Lord's "servant." Not every follower of God is called the Lord's servant. Abraham is called the Lord's servant (Gen 26:24), Moses is called God's servant (Exod 14:31; Deut 34:5; Josh 1:2), and David (2 Sam 7:5,8) and Isaiah (Isa 20:3) are called God's servant. Jesus is the quintessential servant of the Lord (Isa 53). The servant of God is a status in God's eyes to which we should all aspire. It speaks of a tender, close, and affectionate relationship with our Lord.

Why does the servant call on his God for aid? According to verse 17, it is "so that I might live; then I will keep your word." Jesus teaches us this same truth in Matthew 4:4 when he says to Satan, "It is written: Man must not live on bread alone but on every word that comes from the mouth of God." Obedience to God's Word is essential to the life of the Lord's servant. It is his food and drink. It is the air he breathes. As Spurgeon eloquently says, "Without abundant mercy he [the servant] could not live. It takes great grace to keep a saint alive" (*Treasury*, 171). That great grace of God that sustains our lives is ours through the Word of God.

His Word Is Wondrous to God's Servant (119:18)

Three important truths appear in this amazing verse. First, there are wonderful or "wondrous things" in God's Torah, his Word. There are amazing, beautiful, captivating, delightful, excellent, and fantastic things in God's Word. Second, we need God to open our eyes to contemplate these wondrous things (cf. Luke 24:13-35). We need God to remove the blinders, to take away any hindrance to our seeing the wonders of the Bible. Third, we must pray, asking God for spiritual and supernatural illumination to help us see what is there. John Piper captures well the thrust of this verse:

> If God does not open our eyes, we will not see the wonder of the Word. We are not naturally able to see spiritual beauty. When we read the Bible without the help of God, the glory of God in the teachings and events of the Bible is like the sun shining in the face of a blind man. Not that you can't construe its surface meaning, but you can't see the wonder, the beauty, the glory of it such that it wins your heart. . . . We must pray to God for supernatural illumination when we read the Bible. ("Open My Eyes That I May See")

Ask God to Help You Stay Faithful in a World That Is Not Your Home

PSALM 119:19-20

This world, "this present evil age" (Gal 1:4), is not our home. We are foreigners, sojourners, and aliens in a strange and hostile land. First Peter 1:1 calls us "exiles," and 1 Peter 2:11 says we are "strangers and exiles." Colossians 1:13 puts things in proper perspective: "[God] has rescued us from the domain of darkness and transferred us into the kingdom of the Son he loves." Hebrews 13:14 says, "We do not have an enduring city here; instead, we seek the one to come." The city the author of Hebrews has in mind is the new Jerusalem, described in Revelation 21–22.

This world is not our home. We are citizens of a different kingdom. We have a different spiritual address and destiny! Still, we are in this world now. We live in this evil age now. We want to be faithful to our true King and his kingdom now. And we need his help. We need his perspective. How do we get there and stay there?

Know Who You Are: A Person Headed to a Different Kingdom (119:19)

The psalmist says, "I am a resident alien ["sojourner" ESV] on the earth." He accurately recognizes his proper residence and status in this life. He is not surprised that he feels out of place. There is a "spiritual dislocation" he should feel. As *The Message* helpfully paraphrases, "I'm a stranger in these parts."

As a sojourner or resident alien in this world, he needs guidance, "clear directions" (*The Message*). He needs an accurate road map to navigate this world on the way to the heavenly kingdom, which is his real home. Therefore, he prays, "Do not hide your commands from me." This is a negative way of expressing the truth of verse 18. If the Lord does not open his eyes to see the wondrous things in his Word, they will be hidden from him. The psalmist will not know how to get home without the Lord's Word. Philippians 3:20 reminds us that "our citizenship is in heaven." That is where we are headed. That is our home. His Word, illuminated by his Spirit, will safely get us there.

Know What You Need: A Passion for the Word (119:20)

The plea of verse 19 intensifies in verse 20. When it comes to the psalmist's need for the Lord's Word—his rules, his decrees, and his decisions—"I am continually overcome with longing." The idea is that he is broken and crushed to pieces. He is shattered by the internal intensity of his longing. He is close to the breaking point and will not make it without the Lord's Word. This longing is like the passion in Psalm 42:1-2: "As a deer longs for flowing streams, so I long for you, God. I thirst for God, the living God." Spurgeon says,

> The desires of gracious men after holiness are intense,—they cause a wear of heart, a straining of the mind, till it feels ready to snap with the heavenly pull. . . . What a blessing it is when all our desires are after the things of God. (*Treasury*, 173)

Do not miss that the longing and consuming of our souls persists at all times. Our passion for the Word is not periodic or episodic! We long continually to know, live, and keep this Word.

Ask God to Help You When Others Oppose You

PSALM 119:21-24

Opposition should never surprise the disciple of Jesus Christ. Jesus promised this would be our experience. In his Upper Room Discourse on the night before his passion, our Lord said in John 15:18-20,

> If the world hates you, understand that it hated me before it hated you. If you were of the world, the world would love you as its own. However, because you are not of the world, but I have chosen you out of it, the world hates you. Remember the word I spoke to you: "A servant is not greater than his master." If they persecuted me, they will also persecute you.

Paul adds in 2 Timothy 3:12, "In fact, all who want to live a godly life in Christ Jesus will be persecuted." So prepare yourself. This fallen world will not like you or love you. They will not applaud you as you live for Christ and keep his Word (v. 17). They will not celebrate the words and works of the real Jesus revealed in the Bible. Opposition is coming. We should expect it. What then is our proper, Christ-honoring response when it does? The psalmist provides two clear principles to guide us.

Trust that God Will Deal with the Arrogant and Disobedient (119:21)

The psalmist has great confidence in the character and ways of God. He is confident that God will deal effectively with those he describes as "arrogant" ("insolent" ESV), "the ones under a curse" ("accursed ones" ESV), and "who wander from your commands." These are people who do not care about God and what he thinks. What does God do with such persons? He rebukes them. Allen Ross points out that the word "rebuke" refers to "a verbal activity that causes an effective end to the activities" (*Psalms*, 485). We would say that God stops them in their tracks. He puts them in their place. By his powerful and effective word, he ends their arrogant activities. We do not have to lift a finger. Our God simply says the word, and it is done.

Trust that God Will Hear Your Prayers for Relief from Persecution (119:22-24)

Verses 22-24 hang together because the psalmist makes a promise about his relationship to God's Word at the end of each one. In other words, he realizes he is not a passive agent in this drama between good and evil. He has a twofold assignment. First, he prays: "Take insult and contempt away from me." He asks the Lord to remove, like a covering that smothers him, the insults and contemptible words that are on the verge of shutting him down, causing him to consider giving up and dropping out of the race. Second, he must rightly relate to God's Word in faith and obedience.

While you trust him, keep his testimonies (v. 22). The psalmist asks the Lord personally to take away "insult" ("scorn" ESV) and "contempt." He asks the Lord to remove ridicule, reproach, and the taunts of the prideful and arrogant from his life. There is a basis for his request: "I have kept your decrees." When they opposed him, he obeyed the Lord. When they put him down, he kept looking up to God. They told him to walk away from his God, but he chose to keep walking with him. He chose to obey God rather than listen to men.

While you trust him, meditate on his statutes (v. 23). Powerful people of authority and influence were plotting against the Lord's servant. They were in their seats of power plotting against God's man. Echoes of our Lord's betrayal reverberate in the distance. In response, the servant of the Lord will meditate on the Word ("your statutes"). He will not fight back or retaliate. He trusts the Word and the God of the Word. He will remain loyal to the Lord, soak in his Word, and trust the Lord to take care of things. Never forget: we do not fight spiritual battles the world's way!

While you trust him, delight in his counsel (v. 24). The Word saves, it sustains, and it will lead us home (v. 19). The psalmist concludes stanza *Gimel* with a twofold affirmation: "Your decrees are my delight and my counselors." He finds joy in the Lord's Word, and he finds wisdom in his Word. It inspires his soul, and it informs his mind. The Word is like a band of brothers who counsel and guide him. With God's decrees as literally the "men of my counsel," he will pay no attention to those who want to see him fail and who want to take him down. He knows the trials will come. But the psalmist knows the Lord's decrees will guide him in his ways as he makes his way home.

Conclusion

As a faithful follower of Jesus, it is inevitable that you will face opposition, ridicule, criticism, and conspiracies of censure like our Lord did. When that happens, let these verses be your guide. As God's servant, value what he thinks more than what others think. As his servant, delight in his counsel, meditate on his statutes, let your soul be consumed with his Word, and trust him to take care of your enemies. There are wondrous things in his Word. He will show you. He will help you. He will deliver you. He did it for his Son. He will do it for you too!

Reflect and Discuss

1. If those who do not follow God's Word still thrive in this life, then what does it mean to have life by obeying God's Word?
2. In what ways is our need for God to open our eyes to the beauty of his Word like our need for God to give us faith in Jesus?
3. What are some implications for daily Bible reading if you need God to open your eyes to see his Word as wondrous?
4. How does being a stranger and alien, as the Bible says, affect the way you think about the current place you live? What does it look like to live as a "resident alien" on earth?
5. How does being a stranger and alien affect the way you value material possessions?
6. Think about the objects or events you have desired. Why did you desire those and how does this help you understand why you may or may not be longing for the Word?
7. Why would obedience to God's Word result in persecution?
8. If you are not being persecuted, would you still need to pray for God to deal with the arrogant and to bring relief?
9. A common objection to belief in God is the presence of evil in the world. How does this psalm help you respond to that objection?
10. How does Jesus's resurrection encourage you to keep, meditate on, and delight in God's Word while you wait for him to bring relief from persecution?

When You're Down and Troubled and You Need Some Loving Care

PSALM 119:25-32

Main Idea: To gain spiritual freedom, run to the Word and ask the Lord for strength.

I. Ask the Lord to Revive Your Soul and Give You Understanding (119:25-27).
   - A. Ask him to teach you his Word (119:25-26).
   - B. Meditate on his wondrous works (119:27).

II. Ask the Lord to Sustain You and Guide You in a Life of Integrity (119:28-29).
   - A. Ask the Lord to strengthen you from his Word (119:28).
   - B. Ask the Lord to lead you to live faithfully (119:29).

III. Ask the Lord to Keep You from Shame and to Gladden Your Heart (119:30-32).
   - A. Choose faithfulness (119:30).
   - B. Set your mind on the Word (119:30).
   - C. Cling to the Word (119:31).
   - D. Run faithfully (119:32).

The title of this section paraphrases the opening words of the song "You've Got a Friend," made popular by both Carole King and James Taylor in the early '70s. The words capture well the theme of stanza *Daleth* (ד) in the beautiful acrostic Psalm 119.

The psalmist is down and discouraged. He may even be experiencing a life-or-death situation. His cry is deep and heartfelt: "My life is down in the dust" (v. 25); "I am weary from grief" (v. 28). The ESV has, "My soul clings to the dust" and "My soul melts away for sorrow." He is at the end of himself and has nowhere to look but to his God. He is determined to draw near, and he is confident his God will draw near to him, broadening his understanding and setting his heart free from his difficulties, troubles, and worries (v. 32). This psalm shows us several key steps to gain spiritual freedom.

Ask the Lord to Revive Your Soul and Give You Understanding

PSALM 119:25-27

Being honest before the Lord is always a wise course of action. As the omniscient God who knows everything, he is already fully aware of your circumstances and situation. When you are disappointed, tell him. When you are hurting, open your heart and pour out your sorrow. Acknowledge your need for him and the healing and reviving power of his Word.

Ask Him to Teach You His Word (119:25-26)

The psalmist begins by describing his deathlike circumstances. He laments, "My life is down in the dust." He is down and nearly done. All hope for life is almost gone. Because of what follows, his problem does not appear to be physical. Rather, his problem is people—people who would lead him down a wrong path (v. 29) and put him to shame (v. 31). Therefore, he prays that the Lord would give him life and revive or renew him "through your word." Further, in explaining his situation to the Lord ("I told you about my life"), the Lord answered. He is asking the Lord again to renew him and to do so by teaching him his statutes. God's Word will strengthen him and help him make sense of life and the difficulties he is facing. God's Word will help him see things in proper perspective.

Meditate on His Wondrous Works (119:27)

The way of understanding is often the way of meditation. It comes by putting our troubles in the context of God's Word. In other words, the more we know the Word, the more life will make sense with its ebb and flow, with its good times and challenging times. This truth is why the psalmist continues his prayer in verse 27, asking the Lord to help him "understand the meaning of your precepts." And as he gains more understanding, he will meditate and reflect on the Lord's wondrous works again and again (cf. v. 18) (Ross, *Psalms*, 491). Being reminded of God's faithfulness in the past to Israel and to him personally, he can be confident and assured that God will remain faithful today and in the future. Luther said, "'To be exercised in wondrous works' means to discuss, speak, and debate the words of Christ and 'chirp' them to each other sweetly and swiftly, like the little birds" (*Lectures on the Psalms II*, 437).

Ask the Lord to Sustain You and Guide You in a Life of Integrity

PSALM 119:28-29

Verses 28-29 parallel verses 25-27 because they begin with a confession or lament of distress of the soul followed by a prayer asking for strength and guidance. The repetition of the same thought in different words may indicate just how severe the situation is. Words like *depressed, discouraged,* and *despondent* capture the psalmist's heart. Spurgeon's words are poignant: "Heaviness of heart is a killing thing, and when it abounds it threatens to turn life into a long death, in which a man seems to drop away in a perpetual drip of grief" (*Treasury,* 191). What is the cure for such sorrow of the soul?

Ask the Lord to Strengthen You from His Word (119:28)

The psalmist bares his soul to the Lord declaring, "I am weary from grief." Drop by drop his life is crying itself away. But there is a medicine for the soul. It is the Word of God. Therefore, he prays, "Strengthen me through your word." In other words, he says, "Pick me up again, lift my soul, and raise my spirit by your powerful, living Word" (cf. Heb 4:12). It is not difficult to imagine this verse being a comfort to our Lord when he prayed in the garden of Gethsemane. Matthew 26:38 records him saying, "I am deeply grieved to the point of death." Our Savior walked this path. We who follow him should never be surprised if he calls us to walk the same path.

Ask the Lord to Lead You to Live Faithfully (119:29)

The psalmist has asked for strength to sustain his soul. He now asks for grace to guide his walk: "Keep me from the way of deceit." He wants to be kept from deception, falsehood, and lies. Ross says, "The psalmist wants all that is false and pointless removed from his life—because he has chosen the 'way of faithfulness'" (*Psalms,* 492). Indeed, the way to ensure that we do not follow false ways is for our God to graciously teach us his instruction (cf. v. 26). The necessity and power of God's Word are amazing. Not only does it change the way we think, but it also changes the way we live. A Scripture-saturated life, graciously taught by the divine Teacher, will have a different perspective and outlook on everything. The spectacles of faith informed by the Word help us see life and navigate it differently from those who do not abide in the Word. The Word of God truly is "a lamp for my feet and a light on my path" (v. 105). It is a gracious Word from a gracious instructor.

Ask the Lord to Keep You from Shame and to Gladden Your Heart

PSALM 119:30-32

The final three verses contain four declarations of commitment and devotion to the Lord. They all start with the personal pronoun *I*: I have chosen, I have set, I cling, and I pursue. What is it that we must determine in our heart, in our soul, to go hard after in our relationship with our God? What is our role in the reviving of our soul?

Choose Faithfulness (119:30)

Having asked God to "keep me from the way of deceit," the psalmist makes a pledge with firm resolve: "I have chosen the way of truth." He shared his way in verse 26. He rejects false ways in verse 29. He now will pursue with determination the faithful way, "the way of truth." VanGemeren provides a balanced perspective in the dynamic between the believer and his God:

> On the one hand [the believer] depends on the Lord for life, sustaining grace, and illumination (vv. 25-29), as God alone can deliver us from evil (v. 29, cf. Matt. 6:13). On the other hand, human beings are fully responsible in seeking the kingdom of God by choosing and living a life of loyalty to God and his word. (*Psalms*, 865)

Set Your Mind on the Word (119:30)

Having chosen the way of faithfulness, the psalmist declares, "I have set your ordinances before me." The NIV has "I have set my heart on your laws." In other words, the Lord's Word is ever before him. It is in his mind and before his eyes. It is his compass, his guide. It is his GPS. Where it tells him to go, he will go. Even when others (or even his own heart) tell him to pursue a different course or direction, he will trust the Lord's Word amid the fog and haze of life because he knows in time the way will be clear.

Cling to the Word (119:31)

In verse 25 our songwriter's soul clings to the dust, to death. Here in verse 31 he is determined that he will cling (hold on strong) to the Lord's decrees. Though he felt as if death had a strong grip on his soul, he proclaims, "I cling to your decrees." The psalmist uses the personal, covenantal name of God, *Yahweh*, which appears in most English Bibles as "LORD." Life's circumstances may tempt us to lose our grip on things, but we can choose to grab hold of our Lord and his Word and never let go. He will give us life (v. 25), he will strengthen us (v. 28), he will teach us (vv. 26,29), and he will not let us be put to shame. Others may fail us, but our God will not. He will never let us down!

Run Faithfully (119:32)

This stanza ends on a note of commitment and confidence. There is an eagerness to honor the Lord made evident by the promise, "I pursue the way of your commands" (cf. Heb 12:1-2). In other words, "I will not just walk; I will *run* after your Word!" There will be a delightful, enthusiastic, and joyful passion for you and your Word, the psalmist says. And he acknowledges that his ability to do this depends on the Lord. All of this will come to fruition "for you [LORD] broaden my understanding" ("when you enlarge my heart" ESV). As the Lord lifts the burdens of life through our soaking in his Word, our hearts and minds are set free from difficulties and troubles. We are free to run hard after our God and his way. Spurgeon puts it beautifully:

> The feet soon run when the heart is free and energetic. Let the affections be aroused and eagerly set on divine things, and our actions will be full of force, swiftness, and delight. God must work in us first, and then we shall will and do according to his good pleasure. . . . Our running is the spontaneous leaping forward of a mind which has been set free by the hand of God. (*Treasury*, 193)

Conclusion

We began our study noting a secular song that has a similar theme to these verses in Psalm 119. A gospel song complements the psalm even better. It was a favorite of mine as a little boy, and it still is to this day. It was written by a son to his mother to comfort her soul in a time of sorrow and trouble (Adams, *Handbook*, 269). Its title is "What a Friend We Have in Jesus." Meditate on this psalm with the lyrics of this hymn:

What a Friend we have in Jesus,
All our sins and griefs to bear!
What a privilege to carry
Everything to God in prayer!
Oh, what peace we often forfeit,
Oh, what needless pain we bear,
All because we do not carry
Everything to God in prayer!

Have we trials and temptations?
Is there trouble anywhere?
We should never be discouraged;
Take it to the Lord in prayer.
Can we find a friend so faithful
Who will all our sorrows share?
Jesus knows our every weakness,
Take it to the Lord in prayer.

Are we weak and heavy-laden,
Cumbered with a load of care?
Precious Savior, still our refuge;
Take it to the Lord in prayer.
Do thy friends despise, forsake thee?
Take it to the Lord in prayer.
In His arms He'll take and shield thee;
Thou wilt find a solace there.

Reflect and Discuss

1. What are the normal sources of relief people seek out for help when they are facing a challenging situation? Does the Bible support or challenge these things?
2. What is meditation? What does it mean to meditate on God's works and Word? Is this a private or corporate act?
3. Why does meditation help when you are experiencing something difficult?

4. How can your prayers help you diagnose your spiritual life? Do your prayers reveal that you live a life that needs God to give you strength?
5. How do the psalmist's requests to keep his ways from deceit and to give him instruction parallel and complement one another?
6. What are some past examples where you have had to choose "the way of truth"? Are there any present areas in your life where you need to do this again?
7. How is the Bible able to be your compass and guide if it does not specifically address many situations you will meet?
8. The psalmist uses God's covenant name (Yahweh) in this stanza. How does this special relationship with God affect how a Christian can go to him during distress?
9. What are some of the examples in the New Testament where you see Jesus clinging to God's Word to give him strength?
10. How is the psalmist able to view God's commands as something he eagerly wants to follow instead of something he begrudgingly follows?

A Prayer to Live Well and Finish Well

PSALM 119:33-40

Main Idea: To finish life well, ask the Lord to teach you his Word, help you obey, and increase your love.

I. **Ask the Lord to Teach You (119:33).**
II. **Ask the Lord to Give You Understanding (119:34).**
III. **Ask the Lord to Lead You (119:35).**
IV. **Ask the Lord to Guide Your Heart (119:36).**
V. **Ask the Lord to Direct Your Eyes (119:37).**
VI. **Ask the Lord to Confirm His Word (119:38).**
VII. **Ask the Lord to Turn Away Disgrace (119:39).**
VIII. **Ask the Lord to Give You Life (119:37,40).**

When it comes to living a life for Jesus, it is crucial that we remember an important truth: it is one thing to start well; it is another thing to run well for a season; but it is altogether something else to finish well. Thankfully, when it comes to our salvation, we have our Lord's promise in Philippians 1:6 that "he who started a good work in you will carry it on to completion until the day of Christ Jesus." This promise, however, does not negate our responsibility to be faithful in our service to Christ until the end. We must work out our salvation (Phil 2:12). Our sanctification is a divine and human partnership.

Stanza *He* (ה) (vv. 33-40) contains eight petitions that seek the Lord's help in living well and finishing well for God's glory and our good. Spurgeon is exactly right: "A sense of dependency and a consciousness of extreme need pervade this section, which is all made up of prayer and plea" (*Treasury*, 208).

Ask the Lord to Teach You

PSALM 119:33

The psalmist knows the divine Teacher is the master teacher. Thus he begins with the simple and straightforward petition, "Teach me, Lord [*Yahweh*], the meaning of your statutes." There is a note of need and humility in his request. He wants the Lord to instruct him, direct him, and reveal to him the way of the Word. James Boice says this verse speaks of "matriculating in God's school" (*Living*, 44). God is the divine Teacher, and we are his humble, teachable students. This is a school in which the wise person will seek to enroll.

Teach me, Lord, and "I will keep [your way] to the end" (ESV). The CSB has, "I will always keep [your statutes]." Ross notes the phrase may even convey the idea of reward (*Psalms*, 497). It could be worded like this: Learning God's Word and keeping God's Word are their own rewards. It fills our lives with delight, joy, and blessing. Further, keeping it completely or to the end multiplies the rewards! When God teaches, we understand; when we understand, we obey; and when we obey, we are blessed. What a great promise and motivation to press on and stay faithful to the end. Learn and obey the Word, and you will live well. Learn and obey the Word, and you will finish well.

Ask the Lord to Give You Understanding

PSALM 119:34

This verse continues the theme of instruction, learning, and teaching. Having asked the Lord to be his Teacher (v. 33), he now asks the Lord to "help me understand your instruction." In other words, he asks the Lord to help him apply his Word in everyday life. The result is clear: he will obey it and follow it with his whole heart. The idea is with all that he is, he will keep and joyfully (from the heart) obey the Lord's Word. He will hold nothing back. He wants God's Word, God's statutes, God's instruction, to have its way with him.

Once again the Scriptures confront us with the reality of how important it is to love God well with our minds (Rom 12:2; Phil 2:5). Win the battles of the mind, and you will win the battles of the Christian life. Lose the battles of the mind, and you will lose everywhere else as well. Pastor Boice is right on target when he quotes John Stott:

> Stott argues that anti-intellectualism is "part of the fashion of the world and therefore a form of worldliness." He asks pointedly, "Has God created us rational beings, and shall we deny our humanity which he has given us? Has God spoken to us, and shall we not listen to his words? Has God renewed our mind through Christ, and shall we not think with it?" (Boice, *Living*, 48)

Ask the Lord to Lead You

PSALM 119:35

The Lord has taught us (v. 33) and given us understanding (v. 34). Now comes the petition: "Help me stay on the path of your commands." Why? Because, having been taught and given understanding of your Word, "I take pleasure in it." The progression of this argument is amazing because it is so true to our experience. God teaches us his Word, and through reflection, meditation, and study, we grow in our understanding of it. We see how the Word works in real life as we keep it and observe it with our whole heart. But we need help daily to obey it. We need the Lord not only to teach us; we need him also to lead us. Specifically, we need him to lead us in the path of his commands—good commands that we have come to delight in and love.

The commands of God are not a burden; they are a blessing. The commands of God are not depressing; they are a delight. Jeremiah 6:16 reminds us, "This is what the LORD says: Stand by the roadways and look. Ask about the ancient paths, 'Which is the way to what is good?' Then take it and find rest for yourselves." Psalm 37:23 adds, "A person's steps are established by the LORD, and he takes pleasure in his way."

Ask the Lord to Guide Your Heart

PSALM 119:36

The issue of the heart is a recurring theme in Psalm 119, appearing several times already:

> *Happy are those who . . . seek him with all their heart.* (v. 2)

> *I will praise you with an upright heart.* (v. 7)

> *I have sought you with my all my heart.* (v. 10)

> *I have treasured your word in my heart so that I may not sin against you.* (v. 11)

> *I pursue the way of your commands, for you broaden my understanding* [lit. you enlarge my heart]. (v. 32)

> *Help me understand your instruction, and I will . . . follow it with all my heart.* (v. 34)

Here the psalmist asks the Lord to "turn my heart to your decrees and not to dishonest profit." He is asking the Lord to cause his desires to be inclined toward the Lord's Word and the Lord's faithful acts in his life. He does not want to be deceived and seduced by unjust gain. In other words, the psalmist says, "Lord, I want a heart like yours, not a heart like worldly people who exploit and take advantage of others, especially the poor. I need your Word as a medicine, a healing balm for my heart." Spurgeon says, "He who is covetous is of the race of Judas, and will in all probability turn out to be himself a son of perdition" (*Treasury*, 210).

Ask the Lord to Direct Your Eyes

PSALM 119:37

The psalmist must have known that there is an intimate connection between our hearts and our eyes. He has asked the Lord to turn his heart toward the Word (v. 36). Now he asks the Lord to turn his eyes away "from looking at what is worthless." He does not want to give his eyes, and ultimately his heart, to vile, vain, empty, and useless things. Perhaps he was aware of the truth that what the eyes do not see, the heart most often will not desire. Never forget that sin first entered the world through the eyes when Adam and Eve "saw that the tree was good for food and delightful to look at" (Gen 3:6). Guard the eyes and protect the heart. There is much wisdom here.

Ask the Lord to Confirm His Word

PSALM 119:38

The psalmist now asks the Lord to confirm his promise to his servant, which results in his fearing and revering the Lord. He asks God to act on his behalf so that "the divine promise would be realized" (Ross, *Psalms*, 499). Spurgeon puts it as only he can: "Make me sure of thy sure word: make it sure to me and make me sure of it" (*Treasury*, 211). Because God hears our requests, our reverence and faith in him will continue to flourish and grow. We will fear him more, love him more, and trust him more. His Word is our sure foundation; we will stand on it and not be moved.

Ask the Lord to Turn Away Disgrace

PSALM 119:39

Verse 39 may have verse 22 in mind. There the psalmist asks the Lord to "take insult and contempt away from me." Here he asks the Lord to "turn away the disgrace I dread." Evil men reject and mock those who love God and his Word. They ridicule them and heap insults on them. It can beat us down over time. It can wear us out. It can even sow seeds of doubt concerning the ways and wisdom of God. The psalmist, therefore, makes a request: "Deflect the harsh words of my critics" (*The Message*). And he makes a declaration: "Your judgments are good." In other words, he is saying that others may laugh at and make light of your Word—denying its truth and questioning its power—but he will believe it and trust it because he knows a good God is behind his good Word. Others may despise the Lord's Word, but he will stake his life and his eternity on it! After all, Isaiah 40:8 reminds us, "The grass withers, the flowers fade, but the word of our God remains forever."

Ask the Lord to Give You Life

PSALM 119:37,40

The petition for life appears twice in this stanza. In verse 37 the psalmist prays, "Give me life in your ways." In verse 40 he prays, "Give me life through your righteousness." The two verses closely parallel each other. There is no life or real meaning in worthless, worldly things. Life is found in God's ways, and that is what I am asking for (v. 37), the psalmist says. Indeed, his ways are the ways of righteousness (v. 40). In his righteousness real life is experienced and enjoyed to the fullest. So the psalmist asks God to keep him alive in his righteousness. He asks that God not let him lose hope and drop out of his school of instruction. He asks that the eternal life he enjoys reveal itself by causing him to desire even more of the life God provides. He knows it is found in "your precepts," God's Word. He longs for them and, in so doing, loves life to the end.

Conclusion

The Puritan Thomas Manton is right: "It is not enough to begin a good course, we must go on in it . . . else all our labour is lost; the end crowneth the work. God that made us begin [will] also make us to continue to the end" (*Psalm 119*, vol. 1, 322). This is what our God did in the life of his Son so that from the cross he could cry, "It is finished" (John 19:30). This is what our God will also do in our lives as he directs our hearts to keep his Word to the end.

Reflect and Discuss

1. Why do we need to ask God to teach us his Word? What has Psalm 119 taught you so far that can help you answer this question?
2. What does the commentary on this stanza mean by "win the battles of the mind"? What specific battles do Christians face? How do they win them?
3. How often should Christians pray for God to teach them his instructions?
4. How does the psalmist's request to keep his eyes "from looking at worthless things" (ESV) help you think about what you look at for entertainment (e.g., movies, TV shows, social media)? Are there any principles you can glean?
5. Why does God's completing his promises cause the psalmist to revere him? What promises has God kept in your life that help you revere him?
6. If real life is experienced in God's righteousness, then how would you describe real death?
7. What are some common reasons some Christians do not finish well?
8. What types of prayers do you pray most often? How do these prayers compare with the psalmist's prayer?
9. This stanza mentions that rejection can sow seeds of doubt. Is it OK to doubt? Why or why not? How should we respond to our doubts?
10. Are there any prayers by the psalmist that you have never prayed before? How can you commit to including one of these in your prayers this week?

Be Ready to Give an Answer

PSALM 119:41-48

Main Idea: Cry out to God for help against opposition while remaining committed to and dependent on his Word.

I. **I Will Pray for Help and Be Ready to Answer the Scornful (119:41-43).**
II. **I Will Keep the Lord's Word and Share It with Others (119:44-46).**
III. **I Will Love God's Word and Meditate on It Continually (119:47-48).**

Paul Little (1928–1975) was a wonderful Christian apologist who died in a tragic car accident in 1975. He served with InterVarsity Christian Fellowship and taught evangelism at Trinity Evangelical Divinity School. Among his many accomplishments were two books God has used to encourage and equip Christians in apologetics: *Know Why You Believe* and *Know What You Believe. Christianity Today* lists *Know Why You Believe* as one of the fifty most influential books of twentieth-century evangelicalism ("The Top 50 Books"). In writing both books, Little was obeying the command of our Lord found in 1 Peter 3:15: "But in your hearts regard Christ the Lord as holy, ready at any time to give a defense to anyone who asks you for a reason for the hope that is in you." Peter was joining the cry of the psalmist who prayed in Psalm 119:41-42, "Let your faithful love come to me, LORD, your salvation, as you promised. Then I can answer the one who taunts me, for I trust in your word."

Stanza *Waw* (ו), the sixth in Psalm 119 (vv. 41-48), is a prayer for help (vv. 41-43) and a pledge of fidelity (vv. 44-48) to God and his Word. The centrality, once again, of God's Word is highlighted by Old Testament scholar Derek Kidner, who points out that in this psalm the Word is "appropriated (41), trusted (42b,43b), obeyed (44), sought (45) and loved (47f.)" (*Psalms,* 425). God enables us to answer the critic, the "one who taunts me" (v. 42), as God works in us to rightly use his Word to define our faith (what we believe) and to defend our faith (why we believe).

I Will Pray for Help and Be Ready to Answer the Scornful
PSALM 119:41-43

The psalmist begins this stanza by asking God to be faithful to the promises in his Word. He asks first that the Lord's "faithful love" ("steadfast love" ESV; "unfailing love" NLT; "lovingkindnesses" NASB) would "come to me." Second, he asks that God's salvation—here probably meaning deliverance—would come to him "as you promised." In other words, what God has promised, the psalmist wants to experience. He longs for God to fulfill his promises right now in the challenging and difficult experiences of life.

Verse 42 gives the reason for the prayer request: "Then I can answer the one who taunts me, for I trust in your word." *The Message* says, "Then I'll be able to stand up to mockery." The psalmist is under attack for his faith. Cynics, mockers, and scoffers are ridiculing, mocking, and making fun of him. He wants to be ready to answer them and refute the errors of their arguments and false accusations. He knows that to do this he needs to be renewed and strengthened by the Lord (*Yahweh*). He also knows that the foundation of his defense is the Word of God that he trusts (v. 42). He knows he has no hope, apologetic, or defense apart from the Word. This moves him to pray that the Lord will not withhold his "word of truth" when he speaks. He humbly and honestly confesses that his only hope is in the Word of God ("I hope in your judgments").

God's truth can always silence the devil's lies and the empty and false attacks of his followers. We should never forget that the wisdom of this world, along with its prophets and philosophers, will always oppose the wisdom of God and his Word. Today brilliant minds confront the minds of our college students. Subtle philosophies will entangle them, and clever arguments will seduce them unless they stand strong on the word of truth (v. 43).

However, there is a necessary warning we must not neglect. When the enemy confronts us, the Lord will not give us his Word as our defense if we do not know his Word. His Spirit can only remind us of what we have read, learned, and pondered (v. 48). But if we know the Word, then we can confidently claim the promise of Jesus found in John 14:25-26:

> *I have spoken these things to you while I remain with you. But the Counselor, the Holy Spirit, whom the Father will send in my name, will teach you all things and remind you of everything I have told you.*

I Will Keep the Lord's Word and Share It with Others

PSALM 119:44-46

The best apologetic and defense of our Christian faith is a transformed life that speaks the truth in love (Eph 4:15). Our daily obedience and surrender to the lordship of Christ and his Word powerfully demonstrate the reality of our faith.

Verses 44-48 are filled with "I" statements, as the psalmist pledges his loyalty to the Lord through obedience to the Word of God. He begins by declaring in verse 44, "I will always obey your instruction." And as if that were not enough, he adds, "forever and ever." He pledges to obey the Lord's Word always and forever.

Verse 45, as Ross notes, "adds to this the expectation of living at liberty when the LORD fulfills his Word and because the psalmist is faithful" (*Psalms*, 505). This is expressed in the idiomatic phrase, "I will walk freely in an open place." Such liberty and freedom are his because "I study your precepts." Study and apply God's Word to be set free, the psalmist encourages. You are not set free to do what you want but free to do what you ought! Doing the will of God is always the way of true and real freedom. God's Word does not restrict your lifestyle; it liberates it for God's glory and our good. Thus Jesus reminds us in John 8:32, "You will know the truth, and the truth will set you free."

Such truth is too wonderful to keep to ourselves. The psalmist declares in verse 46, "I will speak of your decrees before kings and not be ashamed." With unhindered boldness we speak truth to those in power, recounting the great acts and faithfulness of our God. When I read this verse, I think of Jesus in Isaiah 52:15—"Kings will shut their mouths because of him"—and of the Gospels (cf. John 18:28-40; 19:9-16). I think of Daniel. I think of Paul in Acts. Speaking truth to power is our responsibility. It is also our privilege.

I Will Love God's Word and Meditate on It Continually

PSALM 119:47-48

Our stanza closes with our author proclaiming his "delight in and love for God's word" (Ross, *Psalms*, 506). God's Word is not a burden; it is a blessing. So the psalmist sings, "I delight in your commands, which I love." The verb tense indicates a present and continuing delight in God's commands. He enjoys the Word.

He also loves the Word—something he declares twice. As tangible evidence of this, he will do two things, one outward and one inward. First, he will lift his hands toward the commands he loves. He will visibly testify for all to see his love for God and his Word. Second, he will meditate on God's Word, here referred to as God's "statutes." Whatever goes deepest into the heart goes out widest to the world. Boldness in witnessing flows from a deeply ingrained (i.e., through meditation) love and delight in God and his Word. Truth moves from the head to the heart; then it moves out to the mouth and even to the hands. The Word of God has captured the whole man, set him free, and given him a liberty in life that cannot be contained. When we delight in God's Word, love God's Word, and obey God's Word, sharing its message comes naturally. We cannot help ourselves. We must speak. We cannot remain silent.

On April 18, 1521, the great Reformer Martin Luther (1483–1546) stood before Emperor Charles V and an examination council at the Diet of Worms. Challenged to retract and recant his writings, Luther boldly and famously replied,

> Since your most serene majesty and your high mightiness require from me a clear, simple, and precise answer, I will give you one, and it is this: I cannot submit my faith either to the pope or to the councils, because it is clear to me as the day that they have frequently erred and contradicted each other. Unless therefore I am convinced by the testimony of Scripture, or by the clearest reasoning—unless I am persuaded by means of the passages I have quoted—and unless they thus render my conscience bound by the Word of God, I cannot and I will not retract, for it is unsafe for a Christian to speak against his conscience. Here I stand. I can do no other. May God help me. Amen. (Luther quoted in Boice, *Living*, 60)

Luther chose to obey Psalm 119:46-48. He knew God would not fail to keep his promises.

Conclusion

Spurgeon wisely says,

> There are three sorts of blasphemies of the godly—the devils, heretics and slanderers. The devil must be answered by the internal word of humility; heretics by the external

> word of wisdom; slanderers by the active word of a good life. (*Treasury*, 232)

To say it another way, we must be Psalm 119 kind of people. To say it still another way, we must follow in the footsteps of our Savior, the Lord Jesus. When tempted by the devil, he defeated him with his humble appeal to the Word of God (Matt 4:1-11; Luke 4:1-13). When the Pharisees attacked him, his superior wisdom sent them scurrying: "from that day no one dared to question him anymore" (Matt 22:46). And in John 18:38, when wrongly charged by the religious leaders on the day he was crucified, even Pilate was forced to confess after examining him, "I find no guilt in him" (ESV). May we also speak and live in such a way that those who would find fault with our faith be silenced because the evidence for the truth of what we believe and who we follow is simply too strong to deny.

Reflect and Discuss

1. Do you always have to pray for God to fulfill his promises in order for him to answer them? Why or why not?
2. If you "claim" a promise of God in prayer, does that mean he will automatically answer that prayer? Why or why not?
3. Do you ever feel it is easier to daydream about how you will respond to others instead of praying to God for help? Why is this the case?
4. How is the way you live your life connected to your ability to answer those who would ridicule or mock you?
5. Is obedience to God necessary for him to help you during difficulty? Why or why not?
6. What are some past examples in your own life where you have seen that following God brings freedom and not restriction?
7. Why does the psalmist give an outward expression (raising his hands) of his love for God's Word?
8. How would you explain to an unbeliever who is not familiar with the Bible why Christians love God's Word?
9. What passages of Scripture do you find most helpful to remember when you are confronted with sin and temptation? What is a new passage you could use to help you in the future?
10. How does hope in Christ's future return and rule help you withstand opposition now?

God and I against the World

PSALM 119:49-56

Main Idea: In the face of persecution, commit to the Lord's Word and hope in his promises.

I. Ask the Lord to Keep His Word to You (119:49-50).
  A. It will give you hope (119:49).
  B. It will comfort you (119:50).
  C. It will revive your soul (119:50).
II. Remain Faithful to the Lord and Hate Evil (119:51-53).
  A. Know that the arrogant will scorn you (119:51-52).
  B. Know that the wicked care nothing for God's Word (119:53).
III. Sing to the Lord as You Go through Difficult Times (119:54-56).
  A. Rejoice in the Lord (119:54).
  B. Meditate on his name (119:55).
  C. Enjoy his blessings (119:56).

One of my heroes from early church history is Athanasius (ca. AD 296–373). He was a staunch defender of the full deity of the Son of God against the Arians, who said God was a created being. Arians are the forerunners of modern Jehovah's Witnesses. The story goes that when the tide appeared to be moving in favor of the Arians, a concerned colleague said to Athanasius, "Athanasius, the whole world is against you." He quickly and firmly responded, "Athanasius *contra mundum*!" which means, "Then Athanasius is against the world!"

In stanza *Zayin* (ז) of Psalm 119 our psalmist appears to feel much like Athanasius: the whole world is against him. The arrogant mock him (v. 51), and the wicked, who ignore God's instruction (v. 53), seem to be everywhere. Yet one thing remains certain: God is faithful and will comfort him in his times of trouble (vv. 50,52). When everyone seems to be against you, verses 49-56 of Psalm 119 provide encouragement and guidance for how you should think and how you should respond.

Ask the Lord to Keep His Word to You

PSALM 119:49-50

When life is difficult, it is wise to pray and to flee to God. That we do not do it more quickly and more often indicates our depravity and reveals that sin has made us foolish. A hurting child, however, can always run to a loving Father, which is exactly what the psalmist does. There is only one specific prayer in this stanza, appearing in verse 49 (Boice, *Living*, 61). Interestingly, the psalmist does not ask for deliverance. He simply asks God to keep his word so that he may obey God's Word (vv. 51-53) and sing God's Word (vv. 54-56).

It Will Give You Hope (119:49)

The stanza begins with a prayer for God to "remember" his word to his "servant" (cf. vv. 17,23,38). This does not mean God, like a human, can forget. It is a prayer for God to be mindful of his word and to keep or fulfill the promises he made to his people. As Allen Ross points out, "The psalmist may be praying for a specific application of the divine promises to protect and bless" (*Psalms*, 510). The psalmist makes his appeal fully aware of the master-servant relationship he enjoys with Yahweh (vv. 52,55). This relationship gives him "a waiting attitude, a positive hopefulness" (Goldingay, *Psalms*, 402). He will not doubt. He has hope.

It Will Comfort You (119:50)

Those who trust in Christ have the sure and certain promises of God's Word at their fingertips. When we do not see those promises immediately fulfilled, however, there can be doubt and disappointment. We ask ourselves, "Will God come through? Will he keep his promises?" God's Word answers with a resounding yes! His promises are a source of hope and confident assurance (v. 49). God's promises should also be a source of "comfort," of consolation and relief (Ross, *Psalms*, 510). The psalmist finds sustaining power in God's promises. There are troubles ("my affliction") to be sure, but God will see me through them. His promises give me life-sustaining comfort. Spurgeon is right: "Comfort is desirable at all times; but comfort in affliction is like a lamp in a dark place" (*Treasury*, 240).

It Will Revive Your Soul (119:50)

There is power in the promises of God. One promise with power is that God will give life, revive the soul, and renew us with strength, courage, and resolve when we are afflicted and going through trials. Affliction is the boot camp, the training field, to make us stronger. Michael Wilcock puts it like this: "New life will always spring out of suffering" (*Psalms*, 201). Second Corinthians 12:9 wonderfully complements this verse. There our Lord says to Paul, "My grace is sufficient for you, for my power is perfected in weakness." Suffering is not fun. It is, however, the place we discover that our God is sufficient, that he is enough.

Remain Faithful to the Lord and Hate Evil

PSALM 119:51-53

When I began to walk with the Lord as a young adult, I was surprised to find Bible verses like Proverbs 6:16-19. My mother had wisely taught me that I was always to love and never to hate. It was a revelation to discover that the Bible says,

> *The LORD hates six things;*
> *in fact, seven are detestable to him:*
> *arrogant eyes, a lying tongue,*
> *hands that shed innocent blood,*
> *a heart that plots wicked schemes,*
> *feet eager to run to evil,*
> *a lying witness who gives false testimony,*
> *and one who stirs up trouble among brothers.*

To hate evil is a good thing because it reflects God's own reaction and response when the wicked reject his instruction (v. 53). Living in a fallen, broken, and sinful world, we should not be surprised by evil and wickedness. Sometimes it is the general evil that happens in the world as in verse 53; other times it can be close and even personal as in verses 51-52.

Know that the Arrogant Will Scorn You (119:51-52)

The psalmist says that "the arrogant" (CSB), "the insolent" (ESV), and "the proud" (NLT) "constantly ridicule me." *The Message* says that they "ridicule me without mercy." The verb "ridicule" could also be translated as "mock." It is related to the word "mockers" in Psalm 1:1. Unbelievers who mock God also mock God's servant. They make fun of him for loving and obeying a God no one can see and who, in their opinion, is not there. Nevertheless, because God has been faithful to keep his word in the past, the psalmist will not turn away from obeying God's Word (v. 51). When he calls to mind the ancient words ("judgments from long ago," v. 52) that have stood the test of time, he will find comfort in them and the God who gave them (Ross, *Psalms*, 511). Scoffers should not drive us *away* from our God; they should drive us *to* our God. God's Word is eternal, true, and reliable. We can and should take comfort in that!

Know that the Wicked Care Nothing for God's Word (119:53)

The wicked mock the man of God. The wicked also reject and disrespect the Word of God. Such disregard for the infallible and inerrant Word of God seizes the psalmist with righteous indignation. *The Message* paraphrases, "I'm beside myself with anger." The NLT says, "I become furious with the wicked." The CSB says, "Fury seizes me because of the wicked." To have access to such a treasure, such riches, yet ignore and deride them are the actions of a fool. It is evil and wicked. Jesus said that a person lives by every word of God (Matt 4:4). To walk away from them is to choose the way of death. The psalmist is horrified by such behavior. The wicked have not ultimately offended him; they have offended God.

Sing to the Lord as You Go through Difficult Times

PSALM 119:54-56

Christianity is a singing religion. We inherited it from our Jewish forefathers, but life in Christ causes us to carry it to a whole new level. Throw us in jail, and we will sing (Acts 16:25). Let us gather as a community of faith in a cave, in the fields, or in a small home, and we will teach and encourage one another "through psalms, hymns, and spiritual songs" and with gratitude in our hearts to God (Col 3:16; cf. also Eph 5:19).

Rejoice in the Lord (119:54)

God's Word is a source of joy and singing for believers. His "statutes are the theme of my song" all my life. God's Word is the content of our songs, and God's Word is the inspiration of our songs. Wherever we live and wherever we go, we will sing to our Savior for who he is and all that he has done. As resident aliens on this earth (v. 19), we are just passing through in this life. This world is not our home, but we should praise our Lord while we are here.

Christians have brothers and sisters all over the world suffering opposition and persecution. Many have found themselves in prison for following Jesus. How does God sustain them? Three things stand out from their testimonies: (1) prayer, (2) memorized Scripture, and (3) songs in their heart language (see Ripken, *The Insanity of God*, ch. 19). Singing provides sustaining strength to press on.

Meditate on His Name (119:55)

The psalmist says he will remember the name of the Lord (*Yahweh*) in the night. The idea is that the psalmist will be mindful and meditate on his name when he lies on his bed. However, the phrase could have a second meaning intended by the psalmist. "In the night" could also connote that darkness is in his life.

Perhaps the psalmist uses the concept of night like the apostle John in his Gospel. When Judas left the last supper to betray our Lord, John says, "And it was night" (John 13:30). It was night literally, yes, but it was also night theologically as the powers of darkness came against the Lord Jesus. On that night our Lord was obedient to fulfill the Scriptures that predicted his passion and death. He kept the Father's law. Meditation on God's Word in our darkest hour is sure to strengthen and sustain us. The Word of God will guide us to his name, and his name will take us to the Lord himself.

Enjoy His Blessings (119:56)

Derek Kidner is right: "Although obedience does not earn these [God's] blessings, it turns us round to receive them" (*Psalms*, 425). Our stanza closes with words that are the "sum of the matter" (Ross, *Psalms*, 513). The psalmist has kept the Lord's precepts. He has obeyed the Word of God. According to the ESV, this happened because "this blessing has fallen to me," which is perhaps a reference to obeying the Word (v. 56b) or to the ability to sing when times are tough (v. 54). The CSB, in contrast, says, "This is my practice: I obey your precepts." The idea of blessing or reward is more likely. The reward of obedience is more obedience. The blessing of faithful service is more faithful service (Wilcock, *Psalms*, 201). Spurgeon beautifully says,

> He had this comfort, this remembrance of God, this power to sing, this courage to face the enemy, this hope in the promise, because he had earnestly observed the commands of God, and

> striven to walk in them. We are not rewarded for our works, but there is a reward *in* them. Many a comfort is obtainable only by careful living: we can surely say of such consolations, "This I had because I kept thy precepts." (*Treasury*, 242)

Conclusion

Athanasius is a hero from early church history. William Wilberforce (1759–1833), who helped abolish slavery in England, is a hero from the modern day. He faced great opposition and many defeats in his battle against the evil slave-trade industry. Several times he became so discouraged he thought of quitting. On February 24, 1791, he received a letter from John Wesley that would move him to stay in the fight. Its words echo Psalm 119:49-56 and draw from the example of the great Athanasius. A portion reads,

> Unless the divine power has raised you up to be as Athanasius *contra mundum*, I see not how you can go through your glorious enterprise in opposing that execrable villainy, which is the scandal of religion, of England, and of human nature. Unless God has raised you up for this very thing, you will be worn out by the opposition of men and devils. But if God is with you, who can be against you? Are all of them stronger than God? O be not weary of well doing! Go on, in the name of God in the power of His might, till even American slavery (the vilest that ever saw the sun) shall vanish away before it. (Metaxas, *Amazing Grace*, 144)

If God is with us against the world, it is more than enough.

Reflect and Discuss

1. Is deliverance from difficulty or persecution always your ultimate need? Why or why not? If not, what is your ultimate need?
2. What is the hope God's people have that allows them to endure persecution?
3. What are some ways God has comforted you during difficulties in your life?
4. How often does God's comfort come through other people? How does this change how you will act when you see someone else experiencing difficulty?

5. What can you learn through suffering that you are not able to learn when life is comfortable?
6. Do the people around you generally reject or accept Christians and Christian beliefs?
7. What are some teachings and beliefs in Scripture that the world ridicules? How should you respond to those who believe differently?
8. Sometimes Christians have held beliefs contrary to the Word of God (e.g., slavery and segregation) and needed to change when confronted. How can you know that your beliefs are truly from Scripture when the world confronts them?
9. How can you correctly express righteous anger against wickedness? What would unrighteous anger look like?
10. Do you know any songs or hymns that talk about persecution? If so, what verse(s) do you find encouraging in them?

What a Wonderful God We Serve

PSALM 119:57-64

Main Idea: Let nothing stop you from seeking, praising, and obeying the Lord because only he can supply all your needs.

I. Recognize that All You Have Is from the Lord (119:57).
  A. He is my portion.
  B. Here is my pledge.

II. Seek the Lord with Your Whole Heart (119:58-60).
  A. Pray (119:58).
  B. Think (119:59a).
  C. Run (119:59b-60).

III. Praise the Lord during Your Trials (119:61-62).
  A. Do not let the wicked stop you (119:61).
  B. Do not let the hour stop you (119:62).

IV. Join with Others in Obeying the Word (119:63-64).
  A. Loyal partners are with you (119:63).
  B. Loyal love is with you (119:64).

The great Greek philosopher Socrates (ca. 470–399 BC), when put on trial for corrupting the young and disrespecting the republic, wisely and with wit declared, "The unexamined life is not worth living" (Plato, *Apologia*, 38a). Psalm 119 agrees. In stanza *Cheth* (ח) of Psalm 119, verses 57-64, the psalmist notes the importance of thinking on his ways (v. 59) and carefully examining his life.

As the psalmist reflects on his own life, it drives him to consider the God he loves and serves. He cannot think of himself apart from his God. He can only conclude that he serves a wonderful Lord, who is his portion (v. 57) and whose "faithful love" fills the earth (v. 64). And because he serves a wonderful God, he will respond in four specific and precise ways.

Recognize that All You Have Is from the Lord

PSALM 119:57

Psalm 24:1 informs us, "The earth and everything in it . . . belong to the LORD." Likewise, the writer of Psalm 119 declares that the Lord and everything with God belong to him. In other words, to have the Lord is to have everything! Everything we will ever need we have in our Lord. Michael Wilcock points out,

> Two great Old Testament words beginning with *ḥeth* must have jostled for attention when the psalmist reached this stanza. He began its first verse with the word for "portion," *ḥēleq*, and its last with the word for "love," *ḥesed*, and thus its theme was practically chosen for him: the believer's deep personal relationship with the Lord and his word. (*Psalms*, 201)

He Is My Portion

The declaration "The LORD is my portion" is personal and powerful. It comes from the language and world of the Levites, though we find it elsewhere in the Psalms too (Pss 16:5; 73:26; 142:6). When Israel entered the promised land of Canaan, each of the twelve tribes except one received a portion of land: the priestly tribe of Levi. However, in Numbers 18:20 the Lord tells the Levites, "I am your portion and your inheritance" (cf. Deut 10:9). The psalmist applies this to himself and, by extension, to all of God's people. To have the Lord of all creation as your portion or inheritance is to have everything. What an inheritance! What a privilege! What a blessing! All we have, we have in our God—a God whose faithful love fills the earth (v. 64).

Here Is My Pledge

To have the Lord as our portion or inheritance calls for an immediate response of commitment and devotion: "I have promised to keep your words." Overwhelmed by the reality of his relationship with the sovereign God of the universe, the songwriter makes a promise (a pledge) to obey his Lord's words. He promises to obey because of love, not obligation. Jesus puts it perfectly in John 14:15: "If you love me, you will keep my commands." God's gift to us is himself. Our gift to him is a promise to keep his Word. Why? Because we love him.

Seek the Lord with Your Whole Heart

PSALM 119:58-60

In Mark 12:30, when asked what the greatest command is, Jesus says, "Love the Lord your God with all your heart, with all your soul, with all your mind, and with all your strength." In other words, God wants you to love all of him with all of yourself all the time. It is similar to how a wife wants to be loved by her husband: completely, totally, always. So how do we get there? Verses 58-60 provides three helpful steps.

Pray (119:58)

Following closely on the heels of his promise to keep God's Word, the psalmist petitions the Lord, "I have sought your favor with all my heart." The idea of seeking the Lord's favor is for him to turn his face toward us in kindness. The songwriter has made a promise to obey the Lord (v. 57); now he asks him to "be gracious to me according to your promise." Such an appeal naturally flows from one whose whole heart is focused on the Lord (vv. 2,7,10-11,32,34,36). What access the child of God has to his heavenly Father, his sovereign Lord! We can go to him and talk with him anytime and anyplace. Only through Jesus is this possible (1 Tim 2:5).

Think (119:59a)

The psalmist is introspective and self-reflective in the first part of verse 59. He will examine his own heart and ways, carefully considering them. This is a good thing for us to do on a regular basis. Think about your life—your plans and priorities. Do they line up with God's? Satan will work hard against this. With a thousand diversions he will try to prevent us from rightly thinking about ourselves and our God.

Run (119:59b-60)

Thinking truthfully about ourselves will bring us to the place of repentance. Consider the prodigal son who, "when he came to his senses" (Luke 15:17), quickly made his way back to his father. Thinking on where he is with his Master, the psalmist declares, I "turned my steps back to your decrees." Was he walking in the wrong direction? If so, he is not anymore. Further, "I hurried, not hesitating to keep your commands." There will be no delay in keeping God's Word. He has determined to run hard after his Lord and his Word. There is resolve and steel in these words. They remind me of a song from my childhood: "I have decided to follow Jesus; no turning back, no turning back."

Praise the Lord During Your Trials

PSALM 119:61-62

Allen Ross is right when he says, "There is something hollow about people pleading for God to fulfill the promises in his word when they pay little attention to keeping his word" (*Psalms*, 518). The psalmist has declared his intention to keep the commands of the Lord. Furthermore, when trials and difficulties come and the wicked try to trap him, he will not waver. He knows he will serve the Lord no matter what.

Do Not Let the Wicked Stop You (119:61)

Evil people want to take the psalmist down, and it appears they might succeed. The cords or ropes of the wicked "were wrapped around me." *The Message* has, "The wicked hemmed me in—there was no way out." Evil hunters have tracked him down and snared him. Exactly how, we do not know, but we do know that the psalmist will not forget the instruction of God. He will continue to honor, trust, and obey God no matter what happens to him. The mistreatments and unjust actions of the wicked will only drive him to his God and his Word. God is his portion (v. 57) and his counsel (v. 61; also v. 24). God's presence and his Word will keep the psalmist running in the right direction.

Do Not Let the Hour Stop You (119:62)

The psalmist declares, "I rise at midnight to thank you." Hassell Bullock points out, "This may represent a daily pattern of piety, like Daniel's custom of praying three times a day (Dan. 6:10)" (*Encountering*, 222). It certainly reminds us of the late-night prayer habits of the Lord Jesus (Luke 6:12). "The psalmist did not get out of bed to check on nighttime robbers" (Spurgeon, *Treasury*, 256). He got up to walk or kneel in prayer. The posture of the heart, not of the body, is the key. He gets up late at night to pray, motivated by "your righteous judgments." A righteous God who has given us a righteous Word is worthy of our praise anytime, including the midnight hour.

Join with Others in Obeying the Word

PSALM 119:63-64

Two ideas drive the final verses of stanza *Cheth*. First, we are not in this effort alone. We have friends or companions with us as we run hard after God. We are not lone rangers. Evil people may try to ruin us and "drag [us] into sin" (v. 61 NLT), but we have a band of brothers to keep us on the right path. Second, our God is a God of *chesed*—of loyal, steadfast, faithful covenant love. No god loves his people like this God.

Loyal Partners Are with You (119:63)

We are known by our choice of friends. The psalmist wants to run with those who run with God. This is his spiritual posse. He is a friend (and brother) to all who fear and have respect for the Lord. He is a friend to all who keep God's precepts, who obey God's Word. God's Word is a tie that binds together those whose hearts long to see God's face turned toward them with pleasure. Friends play a vital role in our lives. We must choose them wisely.

Loyal Love Is with You (119:64)

The devoted follower of Jesus Christ knows God's steadfast, faithful love personally and intimately. However, God's love is bigger and greater than that. Indeed, the earth is full of God's loving care. Whether they know it or not, whether they acknowledge it or not, the whole world lives in this fullness of his love. It is present like the air we breathe. Were this not the case, we would not survive for even a millisecond.

Because God loves us in this way, we want to know and enjoy our God even more. The stanza ends, "Teach me your statutes." The request "teach me" is a recurring theme in Psalm 119 (vv. 12,26,29,33,64,66, 68,99,108,124,135,171). It reminds us of the importance of loving our Lord with our minds. Knowing who he is and what he is like moves us to want to know him more. Where is such knowledge found? The answer is simple: in his Word.

Conclusion

The Lord himself is our portion, or as the *Good News Translation* translates verse 57, "You are all I want, O LORD." And this Lord's "faithful love," his "unfailing love" (NLT), fills the earth. Those who have met this sovereign Lord through faith in his Son, the Lord Jesus Christ, can indeed shout and sing, "The Lord himself is all I want, and his unfailing love not only fills the earth; it fills me!" This is the blessing and joy of the Lord's salvation. This is the blessing and joy God promises to all who seek him with their whole heart.

Reflect and Discuss

1. Why is it important for the psalmist (and you) to remember that the Lord is his (and your) portion? What in this psalm's context helps you answer this question?
2. How should having the God of creation as your inheritance cause you to act?
3. What is the relationship between obedience to God and love for God? How could pursuing obedience increase your love? Could someone pursue obedience in a way that would not increase their love? How so?
4. What promise(s) could the psalmist be referring to in verse 58 (cf. Deut 4:1-40; 6:1-25)?
5. In what ways can you better seek the Lord with all your heart? What steps can you take this week?
6. What keeps you distracted when you pray or meditate? How can you cultivate a less distracted spiritual life?
7. How do you usually respond after you realize that you have neglected the Lord and his Word for a period of time? How should you respond in light of the truth of the gospel?
8. What does the psalmist mean when he says that he did not "forget" God's instruction?
9. Are you ever tempted to repeatedly put off spending time with God? How can verses 58, 60, and 62 help you know how to pursue God?
10. Do you have friends who are currently helping you obey the Word? How are they doing this? How can you also be a faithful friend who helps others obey the Word?

God's Goodness and the Blessings of Affliction

PSALM 119:65-72

Main Idea: Affliction can be good because it can remind us of God's kindness and spur us toward obedience.

I. **God Keeps His Word to His Servant (119:65).**
II. **A Good God Uses Affliction to Lead Us to Obedience to His Word (119:66-68).**
III. **The Arrogant Will Tempt Us to Disregard God's Word (119:69-70).**
IV. **God's People Acknowledge that the Pain of Affliction Helps Us Refocus on God's Word (119:71-72).**

The wonderful preacher John Phillips wisely says,

> The constant gnawing of adverse circumstances can wear down even the most committed believer. Yet, as the constant washing of the waters smooths the pebbles and the constant wearing of the sand rounds the ragged edges of even the roughest rocks, so the unremitting adversities of the psalmist were doing their work of polishing and refining his soul. (*Exploring*, 321)

Our good God only does good things for his servants (vv. 17,23,38,49,65). Indeed, the Hebrew word for "good" (*tob*) occurs six times in this passage and begins five lines of this stanza (VanGemeren, *Psalms*, 871). It is the dominant idea that ties these eight verses together. However, sometimes those good things from our good God flow in the purifying waters of affliction (vv. 67,71). They may not feel good, but they are good for us. Our prayer to the Lord should be that of the psalmist: "It was good for me to be afflicted" (v. 71). We learn why the psalmist believes his affliction was good in four movements in verses 65-72.

God Keeps His Word to His Servant

PSALM 119:65

The psalmist begins stanza *Teth* (ט), the ninth letter of the Hebrew alphabet, with a confession of confidence and trust: "You have treated your servant well." The phrase "treated well" includes the Hebrew word *tob,* which the NIV translates as "good." And who is the one who has been good to his servant? It is the Lord (Yahweh), he has been good to his faithful servant as he promised ("according to your word" ESV).

Spurgeon says it so well:

> This kindness of the Lord is, however, no chance matter: he promised to do so, and he has done it according to his Word. It is very precious to see the Word of the Lord fulfilled in our happy experience; it endears the Scripture to us and makes us love the Lord of the Scripture. The book of providence tallies with the book of promise: what we read in the page of inspiration we meet with again in the leaves of our life-story. (*Treasury,* 270)

Our good God keeps his good Word to his servant. That is one thing you can always count on.

A Good God Uses Affliction to Lead Us to Obedience to His Word

PSALM 119:66-68

Verses 66-68 begin and end with a prayer. Both prayers are a petition for the Lord to teach his servants his Word. These verses identify the Word as judgment, discernment, commands (v. 66), word (v. 67), and statutes (v. 68). This Word is good (v. 66) and finds its source in a good God who does good (v. 68).

The psalmist asks the Lord to "teach me good judgment and discernment." He asks God to grant him wisdom and insight so that he might make good and wise decisions. The psalmist is confident in his request because he is committed to the Lord; he trusts in the Lord's commands. The Word of God is a fountain of wisdom and knowledge, and he wants that fountain flowing in his life.

Verse 67 informs us that the psalmist knows from personal experience the pain that many of us bring on ourselves by wandering away, going "astray" from God's Word. Note the honest acknowledgment of his sin: "I went astray." I did this to myself, he says. God, however, is a good Father who lovingly disciplines his children when they get off the right path (see Heb 12:5-13). He may even use affliction, pain, suffering, and difficulties as the rod of his chastisement. Kidner speaks of affliction as "bitter medicine" (*Psalms*, 426). It does not taste good, but it has a good result. For the psalmist that is clear. "Now I keep your word," he says, as a result of being afflicted (v. 67). Now he knows, "You are good [in essence], and you do what is good [in action]." Therefore, he requests again, "Teach me your statutes." He wants the Lord to be his divine instructor. Discipline was not pleasant, but it brought him back to the place of obedience. So the psalmist implores, "Give me more, Lord. More of you. More of your Word."

The Arrogant Will Tempt Us to Disregard God's Word

PSALM 119:69-70

The devil has plenty of people, in and out of the church, who are more than willing to do his dirty work. The psalmist experienced this up close and personal in the form of lies and false accusations. In verse 69 he tells us, "The arrogant have smeared me with lies." *The Message* reads, "The godless spread lies about me." The idea is that the insolent or prideful have "patched together a lie against him" (Ross, *Psalms*, 524). The actions of these arrogant liars contrast strikingly with the good God who does good. Therefore, the psalmist will not compromise his loyalty and allegiance to God. Rather, the arrogant drive him to the Lord with this confession and resolve: "I obey your precepts with all my heart" (v. 69).

The prideful have no conscience, no genuine sense of right and wrong. "Their hearts are hard and insensitive," the psalmist says (v. 70). There is nothing in them that longs for God and his Word. When it comes to the Lord, they do not care. When it comes to telling the truth, they do not care. When it comes to obeying God, they do not care. Again, in striking contrast to the prideful, the psalmist professes his affections for both God and his Word: "But I delight in your instruction." *The Message* has, "I dance to the tune of your revelation."

Lying about others is a grave issue in the eyes of our God. If you are tempted to think it is not a big deal, hear the warning of Revelation 21:8:

> *But the cowards, faithless, detestable, murderers, sexually immoral, sorcerers, idolaters, and all liars—their share will be in the lake that burns with fire and sulfur, which is the second death.*

Pretty bad company. An awful destiny.

God's People Acknowledge that the Pain of Affliction Helps Us Refocus on God's Word
PSALM 119:71-72

The last two verses of stanza *Teth* are what I call "heart verses." They are verses we should memorize and meditate on. Verse 71 speaks of the value of afflictions. Verse 72 speaks of the value of the Word of God. James Boice says verse 71 "is an exact equivalent of Romans 8:28" (*Living*, 71). There the Bible says, "We know that all things work together for the good of those who love God, who are called according to his purpose." The psalmist and Paul are in perfect agreement. "It was good for me to be afflicted." There was profit in his pain. Why? How? Through affliction and pain he learned God's Word better. He learned more about who he is and who God is. He learned better how God works and what he is doing in his life. Paul again adds a valuable insight when he writes in 2 Corinthians 4:17, "For our momentary light affliction is producing for us an absolutely incomparable eternal weight of glory."

Verse 72 gives us the psalmist's opinion of the value of God's Word. "Instruction from your lips is better for me," the psalmist says. The Bible is the very breath and word coming from God's mouth (cf. 2 Tim 3:16). It is good (*tob*). Others may disagree (vv. 69-70), but this truth is what the psalmist knows.

The Bible is priceless. The psalmist exclaims that God's Word is worth more "than thousands of gold and silver pieces." No words in the human language can capture its value and worth. Spurgeon nicely summarizes, "It is a sure sign of a heart which has learned God's statutes when it prizes them above all earthly possessions" (*Treasury*, 274). Stack up all the gold and silver you can find. The psalmist will gladly walk away from it all for the priceless treasure that is the Word of God.

Conclusion

Pain and suffering are an inescapable reality. Everyone will experience them. Even Jesus did. As the quintessential "Suffering Servant of the Lord" (Isa 53), he was afflicted for our sins. His suffering took him through a series of lies, insults, and beatings culminating in a Roman cross. Yet through it all, he would say, "Lord, you have treated your servant well. . . . I delight in your instruction. It was good for me to be afflicted." Good, you say? Yes! Look at what his afflictions accomplished! Even if we doubt that good can come out of pain and suffering, and sometimes we will, we need only turn our eyes to the cross. The greatest affliction produced the greatest good.

Reflect and Discuss

1. What is your first response to the Lord when affliction comes? How does this compare with how the psalmist begins this stanza?
2. What are some examples of how the Lord has treated you well? How would remembering his kindness help you process affliction?
3. What are the primary concerns of the psalmist while he is experiencing affliction? Why are these so important to him?
4. Does the Bible teach that the presence of affliction in your life means that God is punishing you for sin? Explain.
5. Has God taught you anything through affliction? How has this changed your life?
6. What can affliction teach you that a comfortable life is unable to teach? Why do you think this is so?
7. Do you have memories of events that were stressful at the moment but that you now look back on as light and momentary? What makes them less hurtful or stressful now? How does this help you comprehend what God can do with the worst suffering?
8. If God can use affliction for your good, how does this help you trust him now?
9. What can you learn about the value of God's Word when the psalmist compares it to gold and silver? How would you state this truth in your own words?
10. What verses in this stanza do you see exemplified in Jesus's life? How so?

When Pain Is the Creator's Plan

PSALM 119:73-80

Main Idea: God tests us so that we might learn obedience, lean on his mercy, and live holy lives.

I. God Made Us that We Might Know Him (119:73).
  A. He is our Creator.
  B. He is our Instructor.
II. God Made Us to Test Us so that We Might Trust Him (119:74-79).
  A. Thank God for his faithfulness when afflicted (119:74-75).
  B. Ask God for his steadfast love and mercy (119:76-77).
  C. Trust God to shame prideful liars (119:78).
  D. Pray that God will vindicate you with the righteous (119:79).
III. God Made Us that We Might Live Blamelessly and Not Be Ashamed (119:80).
  A. Pray for your heart.
  B. Pray for your reputation.

C. S. Lewis said, "God whispers to us in our pleasures, speaks in our conscience, but shouts in our pain: it is His megaphone to rouse a deaf world" (*The Problem of Pain*, 91). If the author of Psalm 119 were alive today, he would probably say, "Amen and amen!" In the tenth movement of the magnificent Word of God psalm, stanza *Yod* (י), the psalmist prays during significant pain. These verses are a "prayer stanza"; the stanza begins and ends with prayer, and prayer punctuates the verses throughout the stanza.

As a boy, I grew up singing a precious song titled "Trust and Obey." One stanza in particular sounds like a reflection on these verses. It reads,

> Not a burden we bear, not a sorrow we share,
> But our toil he doth richly repay;
> Not a grief or a loss, not a frown or a cross,
> But is blest if we trust and obey.

Sometimes pain is in the Creator's plan, and there is blessing when we trust and obey. Why is there pain in his plan? These verses give us three overarching reasons.

God Made Us that We Might Know Him

PSALM 119:73

In the *New City Catechism*, a modern-day catechism written like the ones Christians have used for centuries, the fourth question asks, "How and why did God create us?" The answer is,

> God created us male and female in his own image to know him, love him, live with him, and glorify him. And it is right that we who were created by God should live to his glory. (The Gospel Coalition, *New City Catechism*, 23)

It would be easy to think the authors of the catechism had this verse in mind, at least in part. God made us, and he wants us to know him.

He Is Our Creator

The psalmist beautifully states, "Your hands made me and formed me." The language of this verse is similar to Psalm 139:14-16:

> *I will praise you*
> *because I have been remarkably and wondrously made.*
> *Your works are wondrous,*
> *and I know this very well.*
> *My bones were not hidden from you*
> *when I was made in secret,*
> *when I was formed in the depths of the earth.*
> *Your eyes saw me when I was formless;*
> *all my days were written in your book and planned*
> *before a single one of them began.*

With the psalmist, we say, "Lord, you made us. And you made us precisely and specifically the way we are. You left nothing to chance." The psalmist knew, as should we, that we are not the product of evolution or blind forces of chance. We are handmade and handcrafted by the sovereign God of the universe. We are here on purpose! God made us, and he does not make junk.

He Is Our Instructor

Repeatedly throughout Psalm 119 the psalmist refers to God as the divine Teacher or instructor. The word *teach* occurs no fewer than twelve times (vv. 12,26,29,33,64,66,68,99,108,124,135,171). Although the word *teach* does not appear in this stanza, the idea is present. The psalmist prays to the Lord, "Give me understanding so that I can learn your commands." He prays because he knows he needs God's help. He is specific. He needs understanding, wisdom, and insight so that he may learn God's Word, his "commands."

God blesses us with earthly teachers within the church. They are his good gifts and we need them. Still, there is no substitute for our heavenly instructor, God himself. Paul tells us in 1 Corinthians 2:12-13,

> *Now we have not received the spirit of the world, but the Spirit who comes from God, so that we may understand what has been freely given to us by God. We also speak these things, not in words taught by human wisdom, but in those taught by the Spirit, explaining spiritual things to spiritual people.*

No matter how smart or educated we are, we never outgrow the need for the divine Teacher to take his Word and give us understanding. God made us for a reason. He made us that we might know him.

God Made Us to Test Us so that We Might Trust Him

PSALM 119:74-79

Verses 74-79 are "the heart of this stanza" because they are "concerned with the psalmist's present affliction" (Ross, *Psalms*, 528). The theme of affliction is a recurring one in Psalm 119. The important truth we learn is that affliction and pain may be God's doing. It is not necessarily a sign of his punishment. It may well be a sign of his faithfulness. He may be doing it for our good, as verse 71 makes clear. There is gain in the pain.

Thank God for His Faithfulness When Afflicted (119:74-75)

Verse 74 begins with a word of confidence during trouble. The psalmist is confident that deliverance is on the way because "those who fear [the Lord] will see me and rejoice." Those who fear the Lord will see God's faithfulness, steadfast love, and mercy in the psalmist's life, and there will be rejoicing, a celebration among the people of God.

The basis of his confidence is multifaceted. First, it is because "I put my hope in your word." He trusts what his Lord says. Second, "I know, LORD, that your judgments are just." The Lord always does the right thing, in the right way, and for the right reasons. His ways are "never wrong, never incomplete, never arbitrary" (Ross, *Psalms*, 529). Third, "in faithfulness you have afflicted me" (ESV; CSB, "you have afflicted me fairly"). Ross explains this verse well:

> Those who understand the ways of God know that ultimately it is his plan to exalt the righteous and destroy the wicked, but that in his wisdom [and faithfulness] he often humbles the righteous before exalting them. (*Psalms*, 529)

The school of affliction is tough, but it provides an excellent education.

Ask God for His Steadfast Love and Mercy (119:76-77)

The psalmist has affirmed that all of God's "judgments are just" and that the Lord sent afflictions "fairly." Still, he needs the Lord's comfort to live, to endure, and to persevere through the time of testing and trials. So he makes a request: "May your faithful love comfort me as you promised your servant." Let your *chesed,* your loyal love and covenant love, be the comfort your servant needs and trusts you will send.

Further, he asks in verse 77, "May your compassion ["mercy" ESV; "tender mercies" NLT] come to me so that I may live." The psalmist is asking God to comfort him with his steadfast love. He wants God's mercy to take hold of him that he might have the strength to live through the afflictions. Then, with a word of devotion and commitment to the Lord, he adds, "For your instruction is my delight." Even in his afflictions, his love for the Lord's Word continues unabated.

We must learn with the songwriter that the same God who disciplines also comforts. The one who bruises also blesses. The one who takes us down also lifts us up. The one who humbles also exalts. Second Corinthians 12:7-10 provides a wonderful New Testament commentary at this point:

> *Therefore, so that I would not exalt myself, a thorn in the flesh was given to me, a messenger of Satan to torment me so that I would not exalt myself. Concerning this, I pleaded with the Lord three times that it would leave me. But he said to me, "My grace is sufficient for you, for my power is perfected in weakness."*

> *Therefore, I will most gladly boast all the more about my weaknesses, so that Christ's power may reside in me. So I take pleasure in weaknesses, insults, hardships, persecutions, and in difficulties, for the sake of Christ. For when I am weak, then I am strong.*

The Lord's strength and grace will always be sufficient for us if we turn to him during our affliction.

Trust God to Shame Prideful Liars (119:78)

The ones who are afflicting the psalmist appear in verse 78: "the arrogant." The psalmist asks the Lord to put the arrogant to shame. Arrogance pinpoints their heart and inward disposition. They are puffed up, prideful, "insolent" (ESV). Lying pinpoints their outward behaviors. The psalmist says that they are slandering him with lies. In verse 69 he says, "The arrogant have smeared me with lies." They have attempted to take the psalmist down with perverse and subversive words. Perhaps he felt his resolve begin to weaken under their verbal onslaught. He counterpunches, "I will meditate on your precepts." He will stay true to the Lord, he says. He will not crawl into the world of spiritual sewer rats who live and swim in rumors, gossip, half-truths, and outright lies. He will meditate on the word of truth and live in that world. God's Word will remain his guide no matter what.

Pray that God Will Vindicate You with the Righteous (119:79)

It is always encouraging to have fellow believers in the foxhole with you when you are under attack. The psalmist, like Paul in 2 Timothy 4:11-16, felt abandoned. Perhaps for a time the psalmist's friends had been duped by the falsehoods and lies of his arrogant attackers and had turned away from him. So he asks God to act on his behalf with divine vindication: "Let those who fear you, those who know your decrees, turn to me." He asks the Lord to let those who love him and fear him come back in fellowship and friendship. The psalmist is not unwilling to say, "I miss them. I need them."

Upon their return, he will make known to them the testimonies of the Lord. He will share with them the Lord's faithfulness, steadfast love, comfort, and mercy in his life. He hopes this will encourage them. He knows it will encourage himself. What he has learned in the school of hard knocks, he will gladly share with others. The lessons were tough. But they were worth it. In difficulty, we learn things we could learn no place else.

God Made Us that We Might Live Blamelessly and Not Be Ashamed

PSALM 119:80

The psalmist closes the same way he began, with a petition of prayer. He reminds himself of how intimately connected the heart and life are. We cannot separate who we are on the inside and how we live on the outside. Proverbs 4:23 is an important reminder: "Guard your heart above all else, for it is the source of life." The psalmist knows he needs the Lord and the Word if he is to have a pure heart and live a blameless life.

Pray for Your Heart

Jeremiah 17:9 tells us, "The heart is more deceitful than anything else, and incurable—who can understand it?" The psalmist knew well this truth, so he prays to the Lord, "May my heart be blameless regarding your statutes." To be blameless would include being above reproach in thought and motive. Leupold renders it, "'May all my thinking be wholly on Thy statutes.' Wholesome meditation on the divine Word should be our continual occupation" (*Exposition*, 840).

Pray for Your Reputation

The psalmist knew he could not lose his salvation. However, he also knew a child of God could "be put to shame." He did not want to fail his Lord in either the private or the public arena. He knew an important truth: be right on the inside and your life will be right on the outside. Spurgeon speaks well about this truth when he writes,

> If the heart be sound in obedience to God, all is well, or will be well. If right at heart we are right in the main. If we be not sound before God, our name for piety is an empty sound. Mere profession will fail, and undeserved esteem will disappear like a bubble when it bursts; only sincerity and truth will endure in the evil day. He who is right at heart has no reason for shame, and he never shall have any; hypocrites ought to be ashamed now, and they shall one day be put to shame without end; their hearts are rotten, and their names shall rot. (*Treasury*, 290)

Conclusion

No servant of the Lord was ever more afflicted than the Lord Jesus. Yet he knew and accepted that there was good in that affliction and pain. God was being faithful to his word to crush his servant (Isa 53:10) so that the nations might rejoice in the salvation of the Lord. As our Savior walked the road to the cross, the steadfast love and mercy of his Father comforted him. The prideful liars were put to shame on Resurrection Sunday when they found the tomb empty! Blameless in heart and spotless in life, the only shame our Savior bore was ours, not his. Pain was the Creator's plan. But that plan was perfect. We indeed see him, the Lord Jesus, and rejoice (v. 74)!

Reflect and Discuss

1. What is God's purpose for creating you?
2. How should God's purpose for creating you shape how you live? How should it shape how you view pain?
3. Read Hebrews 12:3-11. How do these verses help you understand why and how God afflicts anyone?
4. How does the psalmist know that what God is doing is "fair" and "just"?
5. What is "covenant love"? How does God's covenant love affect how he afflicts anyone?
6. How do you think your relationship with God would be different if you never experienced weakness or trials?
7. What are some ways fellow believers have helped you in your trials?
8. What does it mean for your heart to be blameless?
9. What does it mean to guard one's heart? How can one do that?
10. How did Jesus and Paul view the suffering they experienced? Read those passages of Scripture that answer this question.

What Do You Do When There Seems to Be No Hope in Sight?

PSALM 119:81-88

Main Idea: When pain and suffering come, admit your need for the Lord's help and depend on his love and Word to help you endure.

I. **Admit Your Need for the Lord (119:81-83).**
   A. My soul longs for you (119:81).
   B. My eyes look for you (119:82).
   C. My life depends on you (119:83).
II. **Identify Your Concerns to the Lord (119:84-87).**
   A. I need your help to endure persecutors (119:84).
   B. I need your help to endure the arrogant (119:85).
   C. I need your help to endure liars (119:86).
   D. I need your help to endure the vicious (119:87).
III. **Trust in the Faithfulness of the Lord (119:88).**
   A. You have his love.
   B. You have his Word.

In his book *Walking with God through Pain and Suffering,* Tim Keller says,

> No matter what precautions we take, no matter how well we have put together a good life, no matter how hard we have worked to be healthy, wealthy, comfortable with friends and family, and successful with our career—something will inevitably ruin it. (3)

The songwriter of Psalm 119 would heartily agree. He has sought to be faithful and obedient to the Lord. He has tried to live in a way that honors the Lord. Where has that gotten him? He feels like his life is about to go up in smoke (v. 83). He feels like his life is almost at an end (v. 87). As Spurgeon says of stanza *Kaph* (כ), "This octave is the midnight of the psalm, and very dark and black it is. Stars, however, shine out, and the last verse gives promise of the dawn" (*Treasury,* 304).

There is hope even when we cannot see it. Whether we face hardship, opposition, or death, we do not have to despair; in his "faithful love" (v. 88) our Savior will give us life. Three movements in this stanza walk us through the valley of despair to the mountain of hope and life.

Admit Your Need for the Lord

PSALM 119:81-83

You do not know that God is all you need until God is all you have. This marvelous truth is so often found on the road of suffering, a road marked by anxiety, confusion, despair, disappointment, evil, pain, and trials. The Christian life is a battleground, not a playground. It is a war, not a vacation. We will not make it without God, and admitting that is crucial. The psalmist testifies to his need for the Lord in three specific ways in verses 81-83.

My Soul Longs for You (119:81)

The psalmist begins this stanza expressing his dire need for the Lord. The NIV beautifully expresses verse 81: "My soul [Hb *nephesh*] faints with longing for your salvation." His cry has a clear sense of urgency. His situation is critical as the following verses make clear. He needs the Lord to intervene and to do so quickly. Michael Wilcox notes,

> In five successive stanzas the psalmist has spoken of his ill treatment at the hands of those who dislike and oppose him. In *Waw* he is taunted (v. 42), in *Zayin* mocked (v. 51), in *Heth* bound (v. 61), in *Teth* smeared (v. 69), and in *Yod* wronged (v. 78). Here in *Kaph* he is still being molested by the arrogant. (*Psalms*, 205)

We can sense that the songwriter feels overwhelmed. If God does not save him, he will not make it. The only hope he has is the Lord and his Word. Thus he declares his faith during his pain: "I put my hope in your word." His longing for deliverance drives him to the Lord's Word, and he will hope in it alone. Anything in life that drives us to the Word is good, regardless of the package it comes in.

My Eyes Look for You (119:82)

The image of the soul in verse 81 moves to the "eyes" in verse 82. The idea, however, is much the same. Just as the psalmist says his soul hopes in the Lord's Word, he also says, "My eyes grow weary [or "fail"] looking for what you have promised." He is fatigued, worn out, because the promise he has waited for has not come. The Lord said he would save him, but here he is! Nothing has changed. He has looked, and there is no relief in sight.

Such despair gives way to a heartfelt question: "When will you comfort me?" In essence, the psalmist is saying, "I look to you and only you for comfort; if comfort does not come from you, then it will not come." Spurgeon provides a helpful word at this point: "This experience of waiting and fainting is well-known by full-grown saints, and it teaches them many precious lessons which they would never learn by any other means" (*Treasury*, 305).

My Life Depends on You (119:83)

The metaphor of verse 83 is striking. He is like a dried, cracked, worn, and useless leather wineskin hung up by a fire. The flames and heat of suffering have rendered him useless. He feels as if God is finished with him and as if he is of little or no value. Yet, despite all that is happening to him, he has not forgotten or turned away from the Word of God: "I do not forget your statutes." The Lord's Word remains in him. He is down, but he is not out. He does not understand, but he will stay with the Lord to the end. He will keep on recalling the Lord's Word. What a beautiful truth we see here: asking questions of God and having faith in God are compatible. When we suffer, they often go together. So admit your need for the Lord even during your doubts.

Identify Your Concerns to the Lord

PSALM 119:84-87

Keller writes,

> Christianity teaches that, contra fatalism, suffering is overwhelming; contra Buddhism, suffering is real; contra karma, suffering is often unfair; but contra secularism, suffering is meaningful. There is a purpose to it, and if faced rightly, it can drive us like a nail deep into the love of God and into more stability and spiritual power than you can imagine. (*Walking*, 30)

Verses 84-87 revolve around the cry for help at the end of verse 86. They list the specifics of his despair and distress. He recounts precisely what is going on in his life. He has remained faithful; look what it has gotten him. He is confused, he is disappointed, and he is hurting. I can imagine our Savior patiently listening to his child pour out his heart.

I Need Your Help to Endure Persecutors (119:84)

Verse 84 has two questions: "How many days must your servant wait?" and "When will you execute judgment on my persecutors?" These questions of lament bare his soul once again. Flipping the questions into declarative statements, he is saying, "I have suffered enough. I have endured persecution enough. I want you to do something about it."

Do not miss the critical point beneath the surface of verse 84. The psalmist will not take personal vengeance. He is a Deuteronomy 32:35 and a Romans 12:19 man! In Romans, Paul says, "Friends, do not avenge yourselves; instead, leave room for God's wrath, because it is written, Vengeance belongs to me; I will repay, says the Lord." We may want payback now, but we must wait on God to deliver it on his timetable, not ours. We can lament, but we cannot take into our own hands what belongs only to God.

I Need Your Help to Endure the Arrogant (119:85)

The arrogant, who care nothing for the Word of God, have tracked the songwriter down like an animal. They have sought to entrap him, digging "pits" for him. Note the plural. They did not set a single trap; they set numerous traps. These arrogant persecutors (vv. 84,86) come at him repeatedly from every angle. They are relentless in their goal to take him down and take him out!

First Timothy 3:2 admonished the man of God to be above reproach, a man of absolute integrity. Only such a man will be able to avoid the pitfalls and snares the evil one will set to take him down and ruin his life, his family, his ministry, and his reputation. When the prideful attack, walk humbly before the Lord in his Word.

I Need Your Help to Endure Liars (119:86)

All the psalmist can do is rely completely on the Lord and his Word, a Word he knows is sure, true, and trustworthy. He affirms with conviction, "All your commands are true." Your Word is inerrant and infallible. In contrast, the arrogant persecute the psalmist with lies. Will he fight back? Yes, by fleeing to the Lord and crying out for help! Again, Spurgeon's words are so valuable:

> This is a golden prayer, as precious as it is short. The words are few, but the meaning is full. Help was needed that the persecuted one might avoid the snare, might bear up under reproach, and might act so prudently as to baffle his foes. God's help is our hope. Whoever may hurt us, it matters not so long as the Lord helps us; for if indeed the Lord helps us, none can really hurt us. Many a time have these words been groaned out by troubled saints, for they are such as suit a thousand conditions of need, pain, distress, weakness, and sin. "Help, Lord," will be a fitting prayer for youth and age, for labour and suffering, for life and death. No other help is sufficient, but God's help is all-sufficient and we cast ourselves upon it without fear. (*Treasury*, 306)

I Need Your Help to Endure the Vicious (119:87)

Verse 87 resonates with the theme of both death and resurrection (cf. v. 88). The arrogant have so hounded and persecuted him that he says, "They almost ended my life on earth." Still, he will not abandon his God or his Word: "But I did not abandon your precepts." To the end, he will follow him, trust him, and obey him. The psalmist's enemies want to bury him, but he still believes in the Lord and will obey him. Life, he believes, is on the other side, even if it means death on this side. Verse 88 is just around the corner.

Trust in the Faithfulness of the Lord

PSALM 119:88

The life God offers is not one of mere existence. It is a life of abundance and fullness, one you never had but always wanted, one you always longed for but never achieved. Yet the road to this life often contains pain and suffering. Had you not known God is with you and for you, you would have found it unbearable. The path would have been too hard to walk. In this last verse of stanza *Kaph*, the psalmist reminds us of two companions God provides to bring us home, companions we can be certain will never abandon us.

You Have His Love

"Jesus Loves Me" was my favorite song as a child. It remains my favorite song as an adult. The psalmist has endured terrible suffering and injustice. He has been lied about and maybe even beaten nearly to death. Nevertheless, the love of God is his life. In words that have the ring of resurrection, he asks his Lord, "Give me life in accordance with your faithful love" ("steadfast love" ESV). Restore my life, he says. Revive my life. Renew my life out of the overflow of your loyal, faithful love, a love that endures forever. As Keller says,

> The only love that won't disappoint you is one that can't change, that can't be lost, that is not based on the ups and downs of life or of how well you live. It is something that not even death can take away from you. God's love is the only thing like that. (*Walking*, 304)

You Have His Word

As we move forward in life, God calls us to walk between two companions. On one side is God's love. On the other side is God's Word. "The decree you have spoken" is a declaration of "direct revelation from God" (Ross, *Psalms*, 537). It is another witness to the divine inspiration of Holy Scripture. God's Word is his companion along with the Lord's "faithful love." Flowing out of the life we have experienced from his "faithful love" will be our obedience to his Word. Because he loves us and sustains us, his love motivates us and empowers us to obey his decree. His Word guides us and informs us how to obey. His love and his Word are twin gifts to keep us in the battle—twin gifts to sustain us to the end.

Conclusion

Psalm 119:81-88 poetically and beautifully captures the passion of our Savior. It is a lament that is easy to hear Jesus praying. From his suffering to his death and his resurrection, it is all there. As Keller again puts it so well,

> Jesus lost all his glory so that we could be clothed in it. He was shut out so we could get access. He was bound, nailed, so that we could be free. He was cast out so we could approach. And Jesus took away the only kind of suffering that can really destroy you: that is being cast away from God. He took that so that now all suffering that comes into your life will only make you great. A lump of coal under pressure becomes a diamond. And the suffering of a person in Christ only turns you into somebody gorgeous. (*Walking*, 180–81)

Reflect and Discuss

1. What is the psalmist's "hope" that he mentions in verse 81? Why is hope such a dominant theme in Scripture?
2. Have you had the "experience of waiting and fainting" for comfort that Spurgeon mentions? What did this teach you?
3. What is the difference between asking God questions with faith and without faith?
4. Why is it better that Christians give God the responsibility to judge persecutors and bring vengeance instead of doing it themselves?
5. Have you ever felt spiritually unprepared to experience trials when they came? Why? How can Christians prepare themselves for future trials?
6. What does Spurgeon mean when he says, "If indeed the Lord helps us, none can really hurt us"?
7. If God loves his people, why does he allow them to experience hardships?
8. Is the psalmist trying to earn God's love with his promise of obedience at the end of the stanza? Why or why not?
9. How do Jesus's suffering, death, and resurrection help you endure your present hardships?
10. Does concern for obeying God come to your mind during hardships? How would focusing on obeying God change how you experience trials?

The Power and Perfection of the Word of God

PSALM 119:89-96

Main Idea: We can rely on God's Word because it is powerful, perfect, and permanent.

I. God's Word Is Powerful and Perfect because It Is Eternal (119:89-91).

A. The Word is sure (119:89).

B. God is faithful (119:90).

C. Creation is the Lord's servant (119:91).

II. God's Word Is Powerful and Perfect because It Gives Life (119:92-95).

A. God's Word should be our delight (119:92).

B. God's Word should never be forgotten (119:93).

C. God's Word saves us (119:94).

D. God's Word sustains us (119:95).

III. God's Word Is Powerful and Perfect because It Has No Limits (119:96).

A. God's good creation still has its limitations.

B. God's good Word goes beyond perfection.

In 1978, in the city of Chicago, the International Council on Biblical Inerrancy gathered to draft a statement concerning the Bible's inerrancy and infallibility. The statement contains nineteen articles of affirmation and denial, and it is preceded by a "Short Statement" of five propositions:

> **1.** God, who is Himself Truth and speaks truth only, has inspired Holy Scripture in order thereby to reveal Himself to lost mankind through Jesus Christ as Creator and Lord, Redeemer and Judge. Holy Scripture is God's witness to Himself.
>
> **2.** Holy Scripture, being God's own Word, written by men prepared and superintended by His Spirit, is of infallible divine authority in all matters upon which it touches: it is to

> be believed, as God's instruction, in all that it affirms; obeyed, as God's command, in all that it requires; embraced, as God's pledge, in all that it promises.
>
> **3.** The Holy Spirit, Scripture's Divine Author, both authenticates it to us by His inward witness and opens our minds to understand its meaning.
>
> **4.** Being wholly and verbally God-given, Scripture is without error or fault in all its teaching, no less in what it states about God's acts in creation, about the events of world history, and about its own literary origins under God, than in its witness to God's saving grace in individual lives.
>
> **5.** The authority of Scripture is inescapably impaired if this total divine inerrancy is in any way limited or disregarded, or made relative to a view of truth contrary to the Bible's own; and such lapses bring serious loss to both the individual and the Church. (*Records of the International Council on Biblical Inerrancy*)

These statements find biblical warrant throughout the Bible. They have the support of Jesus (Matt 5:17-18; John 10:35; 17:17), Paul (2 Tim 3:16), and Peter (2 Pet 1:20-21). They also have the support of the songwriter of Psalm 119, who repeatedly speaks of Scripture as that which comes from the "mouth" of God (vv. 13,72,88) and is "forever," "firmly fixed in heaven" (v. 89), and "without limit" (v. 96).

Psalm 119 is the "Word of God" song from verse 1 to verse 176. However, in stanza *Lamed* (ל) it soars to new heights in its praise of the divine Word. This Word is eternal, and it knows no bounds or limits. The Word's authority is settled in heaven. Therefore, its authority should be settled on earth as well! Three overarching themes guide our study of these eight verses.

God's Word Is Powerful and Perfect because It Is Eternal

PSALM 119:89-91

Isaiah 40:8 teaches us, "The grass withers, the flowers fade, but the word of our God remains forever." In the first three verses of stanza *Lamed*, the psalmist begins with a strong affirmation of the eternal and abiding nature of the Word of God. God's Word reflects the nature and character of our God, something we also see in creation. There is a permanence to the acts of our God. We serve a God who can be relied on today, throughout all generations, and forever.

The Word Is Sure (119:89)

The great Reformer Martin Luther is reported to have said of Holy Scripture, "The Bible is alive, it speaks to me; it has feet, it runs after me; it has hands, it lays hold of me. The Bible is not antique or modern. It is eternal." Luther's words echo verse 89, where the songwriter declares, "LORD [*Yahweh*], your word is forever; it is firmly fixed in heaven." There is an eternal quality to the Word of God, a quality that will never change. It is sure and settled in its eternal and abiding nature. To put it in popular parlance, the Word of God is here to stay; it is not going anywhere! It is firm, fixed, and forever. Its abiding nature could not be more sure and certain. We can rely on it today, tomorrow, and forever.

God Is Faithful (119:90)

The psalmist connects the "forever" nature of God's Word to God's "faithfulness" that "is for all generations" (lit. "to generation and generation"). He then makes a further connection to creation, something God brought into existence out of nothing by his word (Gen 1). Ross puts it well:

> "You have established the earth, and it stands fast." God's work is dependable, because God is dependable; and the permanence of the earth, which he created, is an emblem and guarantee of his faithfulness. (*Psalms*, 540–41)

The firmness of creation reflects God's faithfulness, a faithfulness that is as sure tomorrow as it is today. By his word, God created all things, and by his word, he sustains all things. Colossians 1:16-17 provides a fitting commentary on this verse:

> *For everything was created by him [Jesus], in heaven and on earth, the visible and the invisible, whether thrones or dominions or rulers or authorities—all things have been created through him and for him. He is before all things, and by him all things hold together.*

Creation Is the Lord's Servant (119:91)

Verse 91 reinforces the truth of verse 90; then it adds to it. Following the ESV at this point, "By your appointment they [the heavens and the earth] stand this day" is parallel to "you established [created] the earth, and it stands fast."[2] Your creation, O Lord, is fixed and permanent. But then the psalmist adds, "For all things are your servants." What a beautiful picture this provides. All of creation is

> standing by to do the will of the sovereign, as attendants might present themselves before their King (Gen 43:15) with the sense of becoming servants to a lord (1 Sam 16:22). . . . All of creation exists because of obedience to God's Word; all of creation, therefore, exists to do his will. (Ross, *Psalms*, 541)

Spurgeon sums up the matter well: "Both great things and small pay homage to the Lord. No atom escapes his rule, no world avoids his government" (*Treasury*, 316).

God's Word Is Powerful and Perfect because It Gives Life

PSALM 119:92-95

Afflictions, opposition, pain, persecution, and suffering are often the experiences of God's children. They are things we can all expect, things that should not surprise us. This biblical truth exposes the damnable lie of what is called "the prosperity gospel," a gospel that is no gospel at all. With its promise of health and wealth to all who have the faith to claim it, the prosperity gospel provides an unrealistic and untrue portrait of the Christian life. This was not the experience of Paul, Peter, James, and John. It was not the experience of the Lord Jesus either. Hard times will come. And when hard times do come, what must guide us in our response?

God's Word Should Be Our Delight (119:92)

God's Word brought a smile to the face and a song to the heart of the psalmist. It is his "delight" (CEV, "happiness"), something he meditated on, memorized, and sang. Had God's Word not held this precious place in his heart, he had no doubt "I would have died in my affliction" (cf. vv. 67,71,75). The CEV renders it, "I would have died in misery." When people tried to destroy him (v. 95), the psalmist found delight in the

---

[2] The CSB reads, "Your judgments stand firm today," but the ESV is to be favored at this point.

Lord's Word. In his pain and suffering, God's Word brought him joy! He loves God's instruction. It kept him going.

God's Word Should Never Be Forgotten (119:93)

In a bold declaration of loyalty flowing out of a heart of gratitude for the Word of God, the psalmist proclaims, "I will never forget your precepts." When he is hurting and in trouble, he will remember and recall the Lord's Word. The idea is that he will think about it and obey it. Why should we go to the Word when such occasions arise? The answer is clear: "For you have given me life through them." By God's Word our lives are preserved and revived. He renews and reinvigorates our lives by his powerful and perfect Word. The life-giving power of God's Word is a recurring theme in this psalm (vv. 25,37,40,50,88,107,149,154,156,159). It should be a recurring theme in our lives as well.

God's Word Saves Us (119:94)

This psalmist affirms his devotion to the Lord: "I am yours." This affirmation provides the basis for his short, simple prayer: "Save me." Because he belongs to God and God belongs to him (cf. v. 57), he can cry out with confidence for his deliverance, his rescue. In context, it is clear that he needs to be saved from the wicked of the next verse. The songwriter knows only God can save him, so he wisely goes to the right person. The fool looks for salvation and deliverance through others when God alone can save.

God's Word Sustains Us (119:95)

Verse 95 reveals the source of the affliction he referred to in verse 92. It is "the wicked" who "hope to destroy me." Verse 92 informed us they came close to succeeding. However, they were no match for the Word, here described as God's "decrees." Spurgeon paints a beautiful picture of what verse 95 is telling us:

> They [the wicked] were like wild beasts crouching by the way, or highwaymen waylaying a defenseless traveller; but the psalmist went on his way without considering them, for he was considering something better, namely, the witness or testimony which God has borne to the sons of men. He did not allow the malice of the wicked to take him off from his holy study

> of the divine word. He was so calm that he could "consider"; so holy that he loved to consider the Lord's "testimonies"; so victorious over all their plots that he did not allow them to drive him from his pious contemplations. If the enemy cannot cause us to withdraw our thoughts from holy study, or our feet from holy walking, or our hearts from holy aspirations, he has met with poor success in his assaults. (*Treasury*, 317)

God's Word Is Powerful and Perfect Because It Has No Limits

PSALM 119:96

Verse 96 concludes and summarizes stanza *Lamed*. Old Testament scholar Derek Kidner says,

> This verse could well be a summary of Ecclesiastes, where every earthly enterprise has its day and comes to nothing, and where only in God and his commandments do we get beyond these frustrating limits. (*Psalms*, 426–27)

Two main thoughts make up this final verse.

God's Good Creation Still Has Its Limitations

All the perfections of God's good world have their limit and come to an inevitable end. Empirical observation and consideration ("I have seen") make this self-evident. In context, the word "perfection" carries the idea of completion, "finished—and finished means finite, and therefore not at all perfect as an infinite God is perfect!" (Wilcock, *Psalms*, 207). Creation, in a real sense, has a relative perfection being the product of an absolutely perfect God. Note that, in contrast with the pantheistic worldview, there is a major and clear distinction between God and what God has made.

God's Good Word Goes beyond Perfection

The Message paraphrases verse 96 as "I see the limits to everything human, but the horizons can't contain your commands." This is a helpful rendering of the verse. The final phrase of this verse contrasts with the first phrase. Creation is marked by limited and relative perfection. God's commands are marked by an unlimited and absolute perfection.

They are forever and eternal. They go beyond any perfection this world and life may offer. To use the image of Matthew 7:24-27, the perfections of the world are but shifting sand, but the perfection of the Word of God is a solid rock that will endure forever. In response we must ask ourselves, "Where am I standing today? Where will I be standing tomorrow? Where will I stand for all eternity?" The choice is ours. The wise choice is easy to see.

Conclusion

This stanza affirms the preexistence and eternal nature of God's Word. Before God's Word was written down in time, space, and history, it already existed. The New Testament affirms the same truth, but it does so differently. It speaks in light of the incarnation of the Word: "In the beginning was the Word, and the Word was with God, and the Word was God. . . . The Word became flesh and dwelt among us" (John 1:1,14). The written Word and the living Word both stand forever. Both are eternal. They existed before time began, and they will continue when time is no more. What marvelous gifts from God are his twin Words!

Reflect and Discuss

1. How can God's Word be eternal? Why is the eternal nature of his Word important?
2. How can you regularly use the teaching that the firmness of creation is "an emblem and guarantee of God's faithfulness" to remind yourself of God's faithfulness?
3. What are some past ways God's Word brought you delight in your trials?
4. If God does not guarantee material prosperity or personal comfort, then how can the psalmist claim to find "delight" and "life" in affliction?
5. The psalmist calls for God to save him based on his relationship and his obedience. Why are both important for those who call on God to save them?
6. Are affliction and persecution always the means Satan uses to destroy Christians? Why or why not?
7. Why is God's Word central to the Christian life? Would you describe it as central to your life?

8. If God's Word brings the types of promises the psalmist describes, why is it still difficult for many Christians to read and memorize it? What can you do to encourage others in their love for God's Word?
9. The psalmist describes the firmness of creation and God's Word at the beginning of the psalm. How does this affirmation shape the rest of the psalm?
10. If God's Word lacked one of the three qualities (powerful, perfect, permanent) discussed in this stanza, would your ability to depend on it change? How so?

Why I Love the Word of God
PSALM 119:97-104

Main Idea: The Word of God gives us divine wisdom, guides us toward obedience, and provides us lasting joy.

I. The Bible Gives Me Wisdom (119:97-100).
- A. It makes me wiser than my enemies (119:97-98).
- B. It gives me more insight than all my teachers (119:99).
- C. It provides me more understanding than is possessed by the elders (119:100).

II. The Bible Keeps Me from Evil (119:101-102).
- A. It helps me walk the right way (119:101).
- B. It helps me do the right things (119:102).

III. The Bible Provides Me Joy and Protection (119:103-104).
- A. It gives me pleasure (119:103).
- B. It gives me protection (119:104).

In a devotional titled "How to Delight in God's Word," John Piper says,

> Never reduce Christianity to a matter of demands and resolutions and willpower. It is a matter of what we love, what we delight in, what tastes good to us. . . . So someone may ask: How can I come to delight in the Word of God? My answer is twofold: (1) pray for new taste buds on the tongue of your heart; (2) meditate on the staggering promises of God to his people.

Piper is on to something; both ideas find biblical warrant in the thirteenth stanza of Psalm 119, stanza *Mem* (מ). Meditation is mentioned twice in verses 97 and 99. Verse 103 beautifully describes the idea of spiritually alive taste buds. What do you meditate on or daydream about? What do you hunger for and long to taste with the tongue of your soul? For the author of Psalm 119, the answer is easy. It is the Bible, the Word of God. In the longest chapter of the Scriptures, he spends 176 verses extolling the beauty and wonder of the Bible. And now, in verses 97-104, he specifically addresses his love for the Word of God (v. 97). This book is special to him. It is like no other book on planet Earth. He has a love relationship with it that is unparalleled and knows no rival. While there are, no doubt, many reasons he loves the Bible, he chooses to focus on three in these verses. These three reasons provide a natural division for this stanza:

It gives me wisdom (vv. 97-100).
It keeps me from evil (vv. 101-102).
It provides me joy and protection (vv. 103-104).

Amazingly, and unlike almost all the other stanzas, this one does not contain a single petition or request. In a real sense, it is a declaration or confession of faith. It is not a declaration of independence but a declaration of absolute dependence on the inerrant and infallible, holy, and righteous Word of God.

The Bible Gives Me Wisdom

PSALM 119:97-100

We talk about what we love. We think about what we love. We dream about what we love. We sing about what we love. The psalmist is no different. There is an object of his heart and affections, and he is not ashamed to tell the world. In verse 97 he bursts out with it: "How I love your instruction!" Of course the Lord, who is never directly mentioned in this stanza, is the object of this declaration. It is the Lord's instruction ("law" ESV) that he loves because he loves the Lord of the instruction, the Lord of the Word. And because he loves the Word of God, he meditates on it "all day long." Why does he love it? Why does he think about it, recall it, and ponder it throughout the day? His reasons appear in verses 98-100.

It Makes Me Wiser than My Enemies (119:97-98)

Verse 98 contains another clear and straightforward declaration: "Your command makes me wiser than my enemies." The psalmist has repeatedly discussed his enemies in the previous verses. They are the arrogant, cursed ones of verse 21 (cf. v. 69). They are those who insult him and hold him in contempt in verse 22. They are the princes (government leaders) who plot against him in verse 23. They are those who taunt him in verse 42. They are the wicked of verses 53 and 61, and they are the liars of verses 69, 78, and 86. They are the persecutors of verse 84 who set traps for him in verse 85 and nearly end his life in verses 87 and 94. And yet all their efforts have failed because God's Word enabled the psalmist to outsmart them again and again. God's Word gave him victory over his enemies.

You and I will repeatedly face opposition in this life because of our devotion to Christ and obedience to his Word (2 Tim 3:12). When we determine to please Christ rather than man, we can expect to be attacked, mocked, scorned, and ridiculed. And we can also be tempted to fight our battles man's way rather than God's. We must not! We must determine to do God's will God's way, believing it is smarter and wiser than the ways of this world. And we must be sure God's Word is ready at hand, that "it is always with me." If we do not have it or know it, we cannot use it. Love it. Read it. Meditate on it. Memorize it. Keep it close.

It Gives Me More Insight than All My Teachers (119:99)

Verse 99 can sound arrogant and presumptuous at first blush. However, the context is crucial. John Goldingay helpfully writes that the psalmist may "refer to people who do not base their instruction on *the* Teaching," that is teachers who do not base their instruction on the Word of God (*Psalms*, 418; emphasis in original). Mere knowledge does not necessarily translate into insight and wisdom. Having a Ph.D. may indicate you have accumulated a lot of knowledge, but it does not mean you have a lot of wisdom. "God is the great teacher," and his Bible is the great book (Ross, *Psalms*, 547)! Allen Ross is right: God's Word

> is superior to all other sources of wisdom and knowledge. Therefore, knowledge alone is not enough; faith in God's Word and the commitment to obey it is what brings spiritual insight and wisdom. (Ibid.)

Know it and obey it, and you will be wiser than your enemies. Ignore it and disobey it, and you will be a fool.

It Provides Me More Understanding than Is Possessed by the Elders (119:100)

The Bible teaches us to honor and listen to our elders. We are to treat them with reverence and respect. Yet it is possible for them to be wrong, to make mistakes, and to allow their priorities and perspective to become skewed. Life experiences are helpful, but they are not infallible. Thus the psalmist can declare, "I understand more than the elders ["the aged" ESV] because I obey your precepts." If he has to choose between listening to and obeying God or listening to and obeying parents, grandparents, teachers, or elders, then he will listen to and obey God. James Boice gives a helpful perspective of this verse:

> How can this be? How can the writer claim to be wiser than these others, particularly his teachers and the elders? Is this only the boast of some smart young student who thinks he has all the answers when he actually hardly even knows the right questions? Is he a "sophomore" in God's school, one whose initial learning has made him only a "wise moron," which is what the word "sophomore" means? In each of these comparisons the psalmist is thinking of those who appear wise by the world's standards but who lack the deeper wisdom that comes from the [Word] of God. (*Living*, 92)

The Bible Keeps Me from Evil

PSALM 119:101-102

Wisdom is knowledge applied. It is the ability to see life from God's perspective and then to act accordingly. Wisdom is displayed in a holy and obedient life to the lordship of Jesus Christ and the Word of God. It is a life characterized by goodness, not evil. How specifically does the Word of God help us do this?

It Helps Me Walk the Right Way (119:101)

Because of his love for the Word of God, the psalmist says, "I have kept my feet from every evil path." He realizes this precaution is essential if he is to keep or follow God's Word. The Word of God checks our conduct. It provides divine guardrails that keep us on the right path, the right road. It is a spiritual GPS that will guide us in the right way and to the right place. Proverbs 14:12 is a faithful reminder: "There is a way that seems right to a person, but its end is the way to death." The Word of God helps us walk the right path, a path that leads to life, not death.

It Helps Me Do the Right Things (119:102)

To honor Christ, there are some places we do not need to go. And there are some things we do not need to watch, read, or hear. Yes, we need to walk the right way, but we also need to do the right thing. The psalmist, as he walks the right path to avoid every evil way, determines that he will not turn aside from God's Word ("your rules" ESV; "your judgments" CSB). In other words, "the decisions he makes in life [will] conform to the decisions of God in [his] word" (Ross, *Psalms*, 548). The compass for his life is Scripture, and the perennial question that guides every decision is, "What does the Bible say?" Because God has "instructed me" in the truth, knowledge, and wisdom in his Word, we will live a Scripture-saturated life. It guides us, and it instructs us. We can stay on the right road and choose to do the right thing because we listen to the right Teacher! Spurgeon provides a wonderful word of wisdom in all of this: "If we begin to depart a little we can never tell where we shall end" (*Treasury*, 332). If there is no beginning toward sin, there will be no end in sin. Let the Word guide you where you go. Let the Word teach you how to think. Let the Word make you more like Jesus.

The Bible Provides Me Joy and Protection
PSALM 119:103-104

Following Christ is not a religion; it is a relationship. It is not a drudgery of duty. It is a delectable delight. His Word is how he feeds and nourishes us. It is like a vitamin-rich smoothie that not only tastes good but also is good for you. In Psalm 19:10 King David tells us the Word of God is "sweeter than honey dripping from a honeycomb." The anonymous author of Psalm 119 agrees!

It Gives Me Pleasure (119:103)

When we fall in love with Jesus, we will love and desire his Word. It will not taste like castor oil, shredded wheat, or English peas. No! The psalmist says, "How sweet your word is to my taste—sweeter than honey in my mouth." *The Message* colorfully paraphrases, "Your words are so choice, so tasty; I prefer them to the best home cooking." God's Word becomes our desire, our passion. It is sweet, and it brings us happiness, joy, satisfaction, and pleasure. It tastes good. As Spurgeon says, "The sweetness of all temporal things fall short of the infinite deliciousness of the eternal word" (*Treasury*, 332). It is spiritual health food with no fat or unnecessary carbs. It is not loaded with calories—only tasty, nourishing protein.

It Gives Me Protection (119:104)

God's Word is nourishing and sweet to our spiritual palate. It is also healthy and good for the mind. Like spiritual antibodies, it protects us from life-threatening germs, bacteria, and diseases. The psalmist closes this stanza by again emphasizing the "understanding" (cf. v. 99) the Word of God provides. Through the Lord's precepts, his teaching, we gain understanding. God's Word teaches us how things really are, what is really important, and what really matters. It shows us what is right, good, and just. It shows us what is, as Francis Schaeffer said, "true truth" (*Escape from Reason*, 29). It helps us make sense of this fallen, broken, confused, and evil world. And because we love it and delight in it, we should also "hate every false way." His Word exposes evil and protects our minds with truth so that we see things correctly. Thus, we ought to hate sin. We ought to hate Satan and his lies. We ought to hate the demonic and the pain they inflict all around the world and here in our nation. Everything that mocks God and leads people to walk the path of destruction and death we ought to hate. We ought to loathe it. We ought to want nothing to do with any of it.

Conclusion

George Barna says, "The primary reason that people do not act like Jesus is because they do not think like Jesus" ("A Biblical Worldview"). Sadly, this statement is true for many Christians. But could it be that the reason we do not think like Jesus is that we do not love like Jesus? Jesus had a Psalm 119 type of love for God's Word. The Gospels show that he loved the Word's instruction and that he meditated on it constantly. God's Word made him wiser than his enemies. He had more insight than any teacher or elder. He obeyed God's Word, and it kept him from every evil path. He never turned away from God's judgment, and he hated every false way. This was the path he walked all the way to the cross and out of the tomb! May it be the path we walk wherever our Lord may lead.

Reflect and Discuss

1. What is wisdom?
2. What is the difference between knowledge and wisdom?
3. What type of wisdom can the Bible give you that you cannot gain elsewhere?

4. How do faith and obedience relate to wisdom? Can you have wisdom without faith or without obedience?
5. How does a Christian meditate on God's Word "all day long"?
6. How can you prompt your heart to delight in God's Word when you only feel a *duty* to meditate on it?
7. What are indicators that your meditating on and obeying the Word is a duty or a delight?
8. Is having joy in God's Word as important as understanding God's Word? Why or why not?
9. Are wisdom and joy connected? If so, how?
10. If the psalmist has hardships and trials (vv. 81-88), then how does the Word protect him, as this stanza teaches?

The Word of God: A Light to Guide Me

PSALM 119:105-112

Main Idea: Trust and obey God's Word as your ultimate guide because it will sustain you in affliction and bring you true joy.

I. I Will Follow Your Word to Be My Guide (119:105-106).
   A. I trust it to lead me (119:105).
   B. I swear to obey it (119:106).
II. I Will Trust Your Word to Give Me Life (119:107-110).
   A. I will trust the Word when I am troubled (119:107-108).
   B. I will trust the Word when my life is in danger (119:109-110).
III. I Will Delight in Your Word until the End (119:111-112).
   A. The Word of God should be the joy of my heart (119:111).
   B. The Word of God should be my never-ending reward (119:112).

The fourteenth stanza of Psalm 119, stanza *Nun* (נ), begins with a verse many of us memorized as children: "Your word is a lamp for my feet and a light on my path." The verse is memorable because it is powerful. Whether by day or by night, whether in good times or bad times, God's Word is God's gift to show us the way we should walk and the path of life we should follow. H. C. Leupold says it well: "He that uses it [the Word] faithfully learns where to set his foot as he walks along the slippery paths of this life. He need not stumble or fall" (*Exposition*, 846).

This stanza is filled with the various ways the psalmist sees the Word and responds to the Word. When he is afflicted (v. 107) and the wicked seek to trap him (v. 110), the Word of God will give him life (v. 107) and bring joy to his heart (v. 111). Indeed, the Word of God is his "heritage forever" (v. 111), and he is determined to "obey [God's] statutes to the very end" (v. 112). Because God's Word has faithfully sustained us in the past, we can trust it to sustain us in the future, even to our last dying breath. Therefore, the children of God can say, "We will follow your Word (vv. 105-106), we will trust your Word (vv. 107-110), and we will delight in your Word (vv. 111-112)."

I Will Follow Your Word to Be My Guide

PSALM 119:105-106

During Oprah Winfrey's 2008 commencement address at Stanford University, she said to the graduates, "Feelings are really your GPS system for life. When you're supposed to do something or not supposed to do something, your emotional guidance system lets you know" ("Oprah Talks to Graduates about Feelings, Failure and Finding Happiness"). Although Ms. Winfrey's advice is well intended, she is incorrect. Feelings rise and fall. They come and go. Feelings are not always an accurate barometer of reality. Sometimes they are flat-out wrong. The psalmist knew there is only one reliable and trustworthy GPS system for life: the Word of God. He makes two strong affirmations concerning the Word in verses 105 and 106.

I Trust It to Lead Me (119:105)

God's Word and only God's Word is "a lamp for my feet and a light on my path." *The Message* reads, "By your words I can see where I'm going; they throw a beam of light on my dark path." There was no electricity in the ancient world. Traveling, especially at night, was dangerous and treacherous. Spurgeon writes,

> Having no fixed lamps in eastern towns, in old time each passenger carried a lantern with him that he might not fall into the open sewer, or stumble over the heaps of [dung] which defiled the road. This is a true picture of our path through this dark world: we should not know the way, or how to walk in it, if the Scripture, like a blazing [flame], did not reveal it. (*Treasury*, 342)

As a lamp by night and a light by day, God's Word guides and directs us. It leads us to walk in a way that pleases our Lord Jesus. The god of this age, Satan, may blind "the minds of the unbelievers to keep them from seeing the light of the gospel of the glory of Christ" (2 Cor 4:4), but our God, by his Word, will lead us to Christ and show us how to walk like Christ. By the Word, we can think like Jesus and live like Jesus. This is the power of God's Word!

I Swear to Obey It (119:106)

The psalmist believes this Word, and he will trust this Word forever, "to the very end" (v. 112). Therefore, he says, "I have solemnly sworn to keep your righteous judgments." Oaths in the Bible are a serious matter. In Matthew 5:34 Jesus warns against frivolous oath taking. So there is nothing frivolous in the psalmist's words. He trusts the Word of God and the God of the Word, and he will covenant to obey it, "to keep your righteous judgments." God's rules, his decisions or judgments, are described as righteous. They will lead us to make right choices, good choices, and godly choices. They, not our conscience, our feelings, or the laws of man, will teach us what is right and what is wrong. James Boice is right: "The Bible is a light for our moral path. The path is dark because the world is dark, but the Bible clarifies the issues and shows us how to walk through the darkness" (*Living*, 105).

I Will Trust Your Word to Give Me Life

PSALM 119:107-110

The Bible never says that those who follow Jesus will avoid the pain and sorrows of life. Second Timothy 3:12 is clear: "All who want to live a godly life in Christ Jesus will be persecuted." And James 1:2-3 adds that we should actually "consider it a great joy" when we face trials because "the testing of your faith produces endurance." Real life will involve real problems, real difficulties, and real afflictions. When they come—and they will—how should we respond?

I Will Trust the Word When I Am Troubled (119:107-108)

The psalmist is going through a tough time. He is not just afflicted; he is "severely afflicted." His trials are great, even life-threatening. This is not the first time he has been here (vv. 67,71,75), and it will probably not be the last. Does he turn inward, have a pity party, and sing, "Woe is me?" No! He turns to the Lord and prays, "LORD, give me life according to your word." The idea is for the Lord to revive him and renew his life so that he may "keep [the LORD's] righteous judgments" as he has sworn.

Do not miss what follows this plea for life. Yes, the Lord must save him. But he will not sit idly. In an act of worship, he will present to the Lord "freewill offerings of praise" (cf. 50:14; Heb 13:15). Further, he prays that the Lord will "teach me your judgments" ("rules" ESV). Once again, he calls on the master Teacher to be his instructor (vv. 12,26,29,33,63,68,99). Exaltation and edification are the powerful one-two punch the Lord uses to revive our souls and enable us to victoriously face the most severe afflictions. "Life without light, or zeal without knowledge, would be but half a blessing" (Spurgeon, *Treasury*, 343). The psalmist wants all of the Lord, especially when he is hurting.

I Will Trust the Word When My Life Is in Danger (119:109-110)

The affliction the psalmist suffers is almost certainly the result of persecution. We see this when he says in verse 109, "My life is constantly in danger" ("I hold my life in my hand continually" ESV), and in verse 110, "The wicked have set a trap for me." He has lived a life of faithfulness for all to see. The wicked hate the way of the righteous and have tried to ensnare him. However, they will fail. Note the beautiful Hebrew parallel in the second lines of verses 109-110:

> *I do not forget your instruction.* (v. 109)
> *I have not wandered from your precepts.* (v. 110)

The second idea reinforces the first. Because we think a certain way, we will love a certain way, even when our life is in danger. God's Word, which we love, informs our mind and lights our path. It shows us where to go, and we will not stray from its path. After all, it is the path of life. All other paths lead only to death. Proverbs 14:12 remains true: "There is a way that seems right to a person, but its end is the way to death."

I Will Delight in Your Word until the End

PSALM 119:111-112

The last two verses of stanza *Nun* have an eschatological ring. They look forward and reflect on "some of the blessings that come from living a life committed to obeying the Lord" (Ross, *Psalms*, 553). The value and worth he ascribes to the Word of God are impressive. He stakes his entire future on it. The Scriptures are his personal promised land. Hassell Bullock puts it nicely: "In that inherited land of the Torah life, joy is the tone of existence" (*Psalms 73–150*, 365).

The Word of God Should Be the Joy of My Heart (119:111)

The psalmist boldly declares, "I have your decrees as a heritage forever." This is the language of Canaan and the promised land. God's Word is eternal, and its promises are "more sure than the inheritance of the land of Canaan" (Ross, *Psalms*, 553). Such an inheritance brings pure joy to his heart. Obeying the Word always does. It is not drudgery. It is not a pain. It is not enslaving. It liberates us, sets us free, and thrills our souls. The idea of ever walking away from or walking back on his promises is not even a consideration. They are his inheritance forever. They are the joy of his heart forever as well. He treasures God's Word. He loves God's Word.

The Word of God Should Be My Never-Ending Reward (119:112)

The theme of the heart continues into verse 112. Because the Word of God is the "joy of my heart" (v. 111), "I am resolved to obey your statutes to the very end" (v. 112). James Boice sums it all up well when he writes,

> In the ending of the *nun* stanza, we see again that the psalmist was a practical person. The last statement is one of fierce determination: "My heart is set on keeping your decrees to the very end" (v. 112). The reasons he will keep God's decrees to the very end are those he has identified in this stanza. He wants to keep God's decrees because he will be able to live a God-pleasing life, he will understand the nature of true righteousness, he will possess a divine perspective on suffering and will triumph in it, he will be able to worship God rightly, he will not be turned aside from obedience to God's law by any physical danger, he will not be distracted by the snares of evil men, and he will have a heritage that will last forever. (*Living*, 110)

Such a treasure of blessings is its own reward and blessing. It is a glorious inheritance that is eternal and can never be taken from us. This is how God's Word will guide us. This is where God's Word will take us. What an inheritance! What a reward! This world can offer nothing like this. It never can. It never will. "The grass withers, the flowers fade, but the word of our God remains forever" (Isa 40:8).

Conclusion

Proverbs 4:18-19 teaches us,

> *The path of the righteous is like the light of dawn,*
> *shining brighter and brighter until midday.*
> *But the way of the wicked is like the darkest gloom;*
> *they don't know what makes them stumble.*

The written Word points us to the living Word, the Lord Jesus Christ, who said, "I am the light of the world. Anyone who follows me will never walk in the darkness but will have the light of life" (John 8:12). If we follow this theme throughout Scripture, we can understand why the apostle John would write, "If we walk in the light as he himself is in the light, we have fellowship with one another, and the blood of Jesus his Son cleanses us from all sin" (1 John 1:7). Our world is a terrible world of darkness. God's Word, however, is a wonderful world of light.

Reflect and Discuss

1. Why are feelings not always the best indicator of what you are supposed to do? Does this mean we should discount our feelings? Why or why not?
2. In what ways can God's Word be a guide for your life on the issues that it does not directly address?
3. The psalmist commits himself to keep God's judgments. How can making a prior commitment to obey God help you obey when you are in the middle of a decision?
4. What type of "life" does God's Word bring to those who are physically and mentally afflicted?
5. David responds to his affliction with praise. What in Psalm 119 can help you understand why he does this?
6. Who else in Scripture responds to affliction with trust in God and his Word? How can their response encourage us?
7. Does holding Scripture as "the joy of your heart" require that you have a certain feeling every time you read Scripture? Why or why not?
8. How can you properly evaluate whether God's Word is the joy of your heart? How can other Christians help you evaluate your heart?
9. What should Christians expect to happen when they suffer if God's Word is not already their joy?
10. Are Christians ever in danger of loving God's Word without loving Christ? How can you know if this is happening?

How Should We Respond to the Wicked?

PSALM 119:113-120

Main Idea: Reject the life of the wicked, warn them of God's judgment, and cling to your hope in God.

I. **We Should Hate the Way the Double-Minded Think (119:113-114).**
   A. They do not love God's Word (119:113).
   B. They do not hope in God's Word (119:114).

II. **We Should Not Associate with Those Who Have No Regard for God (119:115-117).**
   A. They do not obey God's commands (119:115).
   B. They do not trust God's promises (119:116).
   C. They do not rest in God's strength (119:117).

III. **We Should Warn the Wicked that God Will Judge (119:118-120).**
   A. The wicked are foolish (119:118).
   B. The wicked will not last (119:119).
   C. The wicked lack reverence (119:120).

The word *hate*, which occurs more than 150 times in the Bible, is a difficult word for Christians. Jesus says in the Sermon on the Mount to love our enemies, not to hate them (Matt 5:43-44). Yet Scripture instructs us on numerous occasions to hate or to reject something. In Christian circles we are often admonished to hate the sin but not the sinner. Though some would argue this is a distinction without a difference, there is a significant difference. C. S. Lewis helps us think through the difference when he writes,

> Now that I come to think of it, I remember Christian teachers telling me long ago that I must hate a bad man's actions, but not hate the bad man; or, as they would say, hate the sin but not the sinner.
>
> For a long time I used to think this a silly, straw-splitting distinction: how could you hate what a man did and not hate the man? But years later it occurred to me that there was one man to whom I had been doing this all my life—namely myself. However much I might dislike my own cowardice or

> conceit or greed, I went on loving myself. There had never been the slightest difficulty about it. In fact the very reason why I hated the things was that I loved the man. Just because I loved myself, I was sorry to find that I was the sort of man who did those things. Consequently, Christianity does not want us to reduce by one atom the hatred we feel for cruelty and treachery. We ought to hate them. Not one word of what we have said about them needs to be unsaid. But it does want us to hate them in the same way in which we hate things in ourselves: being sorry that the man should have done such things, and hoping, if it is anyway possible, that somehow, sometime, somewhere he can be cured and made human again. (*Mere Christianity*, 117)

Stanza *Samek* (ס), the fifteenth in Psalm 119, addresses how we should respond to the wicked. Three actions are highlighted; each relates to how one responds to God and his Word. If we genuinely want to be "human again," as Lewis said and as God designed us, we will heed well the instruction we find here.

We Should Hate the Way the Double-Minded Think
PSALM 119:113-114

In Joshua 24:15 Joshua commands Israel to "choose this day whom you will serve" (ESV). The options were between the false gods of this world and the one true God who had rescued them out of Egypt. Indecision was not an option. Double-mindedness was not an option. You can follow the Lord or you can follow idols; you cannot follow both. God is unimpressed with the double-minded, as James 1:5-8 makes clear. If you are not with God, you are against God (cf. Luke 11:23). Why should God's people hate the double-minded? The psalmist gives us two reasons.

They Do Not Love God's Word (119:113)

The psalmist makes a simple declaration in verse 113: "I hate those who are double-minded." The Hebrew word for "double-minded" occurs only here in the Old Testament. Ross writes, "It describes people who are fickle, who cannot decide what they believe" (*Psalms*, 556). We get a good picture of such people in 1 Kings 18:21, where Elijah dresses down the people who "waver" between following the Lord and following Baal. The psalmist says that double-mindedness is a matter of the heart and what you love. If we love God's instruction, his Word, then the ideas and philosophies of this world will have no attraction. If we love (choose) God and his Word, we will hate (reject) that way of thinking that opposes him. As Spurgeon well says, "The opposite of the fixed and infallible law of God is the wavering, changing opinion of men" (*Treasury*, 355). Only a fool would choose the latter.

They Do Not Hope in God's Word (119:114)

The psalmist loves the Word of God, and he hopes in the Word of God. His love and devotion to the instruction of the Lord guard his heart against being double-minded. His love for the instruction of the Lord also fuels hope as he finds in God's Word both his "shelter" ("hiding place" ESV) and his "shield." The image of God being a shelter indicates his Word is a place of safety and protection. The shield points to God's Word as his protector and defender. The Word of God is a place of safety from double-mindedness. It is also a defense against hopelessness. VanGemeren says, "The ways of the righteous and the wicked are clearly divergent" (*Psalms*, 880). He is right. They do not think the same way, they do not love the same things, they do not trust in the same things, and they do not hope in the same things. It is right to hate the ways of the double-minded.

We Should Not Associate with Those Who Have No Regard for God

PSALM 119:115-117

Psalm 1 warns us about our associations. It instructs us not to walk in the advice of the wicked or stand in the pathway with sinners or sit in the company of mockers. Our companions will impact our way of thinking, our morals, and our reputations. Knowing this warning, the psalmist addresses the double-minded, whom he now calls "evildoers," in verse 115 (NIV). He then pleads for God's help in verses 116-117.

They Do Not Obey God's Commands (119:115)

The psalmist is blunt with those he calls "evil ones." He commands them to "depart" from him. Today we might say, "Get lost!" "Move on!" "Hit the road!" Why does he speak in such a direct, even harsh, way? It is because he wants to "obey my God's commands." The Word of God means little or nothing to those whose life is characterized by evil. They have no respect or regard for it. In contrast, the child of God has a passion for Scripture. He loves it (v. 113). He hopes in it (v. 114). He longs to obey it (v. 115). Jesus, at the judgment, will command lawbreakers to depart from him forever (Matt 7:23). So we would do well to tell them to leave us alone today.

They Do Not Trust God's Promises (119:116)

The double-minded men of verse 113, who are characterized as workers of evil in verse 115, were likely attempting to lead the psalmist away from God. They wanted him to compromise his commitments and convictions. No doubt they could be persuasive, exerting enormous pressure. To stand strong, he would need God's help. He asks the Lord for two things in verse 116. First, the psalmist asks the Lord to sustain and strengthen him so that he may live every day for the Lord. God is his protection and defense (v. 114). Evil men do not trust in the promises of his Word, but the psalmist says, "I do."

Second, he pleads, "Do not let me be ashamed of my hope." The Hebrew word for "be ashamed," according to Ross,

> means much more than being embarrassed or made to look silly; it is commonly used for humiliating defeats at the hands of the enemies. [The psalmist] does not want to be so humiliated and have his belief in God's word seriously discredited. (*Psalms*, 558)

Evil men care nothing for the promises of God. The psalmist will stake his life and his reputation on them. Indeed, they are his only hope and assurance.

They Do Not Rest in God's Strength (119:117)

Verse 117 closely parallels verse 116; both begin with a request to "sustain" that results in life and safety. The double-minded do not depend on the power and strength of the Lord, but the psalmist does. Continuing his prayer, he asks God, "Sustain me ["hold me up" ESV] so that I can be safe." He leans and depends on the Lord for support, rest, and safety. God is his hiding place, shield, and hope.

The psalmist prays again with a purpose. In verse 116 he prays so that he would not be put to shame as he hopes in the Lord. In verse 117 he prays so that he would "always be concerned about your statutes." Spurgeon is right: "Perseverance to the end, obedience continually, comes only through the divine power" (*Treasury*, 357). The psalmist requests divine power that he might honor God's Word every day of his life. What are you resting in? What are you trusting in? Who or what is your hiding place? Continual obedience is only possible as we rest in the Lord—his promises, his strength.

We Should Warn the Wicked that God Will Judge

PSALM 119:118-120

The phrase *judgment day* should strike fear in the heart of every human person. The certainty of its coming is a signed, sealed, and settled reality. Evildoers and those who disregard God and his Word will not continue to prosper, and they will not escape divine judgment. Genesis 18:25 raises the question, "Won't the Judge of the whole earth do what is just?" Verses 118-120 of this psalm answer with a resounding "Yes!" that causes the psalmist to tremble at the thought of what is coming for those who hate God.

The Wicked Are Foolish (119:118)

I often say sin makes us stupid. And it does. Verse 118 makes that point clear. God rejects those who walk away from his Word. Ross writes, "Those who abandon the law of God have no future with God" (*Psalms*, 558). Their disobedience proves that they are playing the fool! Their cunning and deceitfulness are all in vain. It is all for nothing. They may have lied to and fooled others. They may have lied to and fooled themselves. But they have not fooled God! They have lived a lie and deceived themselves. They think they are fine. They think they will never give an account of their evil. Romans 1:22 could well be written on their tombstone: "Claiming to be wise, they become fools."

The Wicked Will Not Last (119:119)

Judgment day is coming. You can be certain of that fact. When it does, the wicked of the earth will be discarded like "dross from metal." Dross is the useless material that forms on top when precious metal is being refined by fire. It is worthless and has no value, so it is removed and discarded. *The Message* paraphrases it well: "You reject earth's wicked as so much rubbish." Such a terrifying reality drives the psalmist again in the right direction. It drives him to the Scriptures. For a second time (cf. v. 113) he affirms his love for God's instruction and decrees. His commitment, his loyalty, is to the Lord's Word. This is what he is devoted to because, as Isaiah 40:8 says, "The grass withers, the flowers fade, but the word of our God remains forever."

The Wicked Lack Reverence (119:120)

Considering what awaits the wicked in final, future, eschatological judgment terrifies the psalmist. His flesh trembles. His skin gets goosebumps and crawls. We might say the thought causes the hairs on his arms to stand up. The fear he experiences as he contemplates the judgment of God is not a reverential fear. It is a real and actual fear and terror of how terrible and awesome divine judgment is. Ross once more is helpful: "The psalmist is not afraid that he might be swept away in the judgment; he is overwhelmed and terrified at the thought of divine justice on all the ungodly" (*Psalms*, 560). Of this reality we can be certain. Of this reality we must warn the wicked.

Conclusion

God hates the ways of the ungodly and so should we. When they stand before the great white throne (Rev 20:11-15), they will be judged justly for all their works. Every single one. They will not be able to hide. They will not be able to talk their way out of the guilty verdict they will receive. Amazingly, although God hates their evil, wicked ways, he still loves them and has made a way of escape possible. It is the way of salvation proclaimed in the gospel and accomplished by the death and resurrection of his Son, the Lord Jesus Christ. We who have believed the gospel and received divine forgiveness must warn unbelievers of the wrath that is to come. We should tremble at the thought of it. We should do what we can to snatch them out of the fire (Jude 23) while there is still time. Judgment day is coming.

Reflect and Discuss

1. Have you ever considered what C. S. Lewis observed about how Christians hate their sin but not themselves? How does this shape how you view other people and their sins?
2. What is "double-mindedness"? What are examples of it being lived out?
3. What does it mean to love God's Word? Is this love an emotion or an action?

4. Is anger ever a proper response to the sin of others? Why or why not?
5. How can you obey God's commands to reject evil people and yet still love them?
6. What are some areas of life other than God's Word that you are tempted to use as your "shelter" and "shield"? Describe a time when you trusted in other "shelters" and they failed you.
7. How can you know whether God's Word is your shield and hope?
8. The wicked are attempting to shame the psalmist for his hope. Why would abandoning his hope, however, bring him more shame?
9. What does it mean to fear God's judgment?
10. Does the sin of others ever cause you to have a feeling of superiority? How does the gospel speak to this issue?

Marks of the Servant of the Lord

PSALM 119:121-128

Main Idea: Servants of God obey and love his Word as they wait for him to teach them and to deliver them from injustice.

I. God's Servants Pursue Justice and Trust in God's Love (119:121-124).

A. Ask God to protect you (119:121-122).

B. Ask God to deliver you (119:123).

C. Ask God to teach you (119:124).

II. God's Servants Ask for Spiritual Insight and Plead with God to Act (119:125-126).

A. Ask the Lord for understanding of his Word (119:125).

B. Ask the Lord to vindicate his reputation (119:126).

III. God's Servants Love the Lord's Word and Hate All That Is False (119:127-128).

A. Affirm the value of God's Word (119:127).

B. Affirm the truth of God's Word (119:128).

How we see ourselves in our relationship to God will affect how we think and act. If we think God exists to serve us, we will treat him like a genie in the sky. If, on the other hand, we believe we exist to serve and worship him, we will be quick to listen to his Word and obey his commands. We will think more about God than we think about ourselves.

Jesus teaches us in Matthew 10:24 that "a disciple is not above his teacher, or a slave above his master." As our Master, Jesus provides our example as the Lord's servant. The word "servant" occurs fourteen times in Psalm 119 (vv. 17,23,38,49,65,76,84,91,122,124,125,135,140,176). Here in stanza *Ayin* (ע), "servant" appears three times, making it the heart of this meditation. Verse 125 is simple and straightforward: "I am your servant." These words capture the essence of verses 121-128 and provide a road map into the heart, mind, and emotions of the man or woman who delights in being the Lord's servant. Jesus was the Lord's servant *par excellence.* It is easy to imagine him singing this psalm. May this psalm also characterize those of us who call Jesus our Master and seek to follow in his footsteps.

God's Servants Pursue Justice and Trust in God's Love

PSALM 119:121-124

The servant of the Lord Jesus has an especially precious and tender relationship with his Master, who loves and cares for him. He can enter his Master's presence at any time, knowing he will receive a warm reception and a ready ear. Our Master loves like a tenderhearted father, and he cares like a compassionate older brother. The New Testament describes our God's relationship to his servants, his children, in this manner in John 1:12 and Hebrews 2:11. With this truth as the foundation for our Master-servant relationship, this psalm shows how we may petition our Lord with a passion for what matters to him.

Ask God to Protect You (119:121-122)

Stanza *Ayin* begins with a confession and affirmation: "I have done what is just and right." I have done justice and righteousness. *The Message* paraphrases, "I stood up for justice and the right." To stand up for justice and righteousness means standing against injustice and wrongdoing. With God's Word as our guide, our GPS, we take a stand for what God loves and values.

Taking a stand for the Lord leads to a prayer for help. First, the psalmist says, "Do not leave me to my oppressors" (v. 121). Verse 122 reinforces this plea: "Do not let the arrogant oppress me." Second, he appeals, "Guarantee your servant's well-being." The psalmist affirms that he has stood up for the Lord, so now he needs the Lord to stand up for him. His enemies seek to harm him and oppress him. They try to shut him up. They try to seduce him and to bully him to compromise. But his stand for what is just and right requires the Lord's presence and the Lord's promise of protection. The psalmist needs his Master to stand with him as he continues to stand for the Lord.

Ask God to Deliver You (119:123)

Michael Wilcock ties verse 123 to verses 121-122 and summarizes well the psalmist's thinking: "I have done what the Word rules (v. 121), but I am still looking for what it promises (v. 123)" (*Psalms*, 212). The songwriter continues his prayer with a beautiful word picture: "My eyes grow weary looking for your salvation." Ross says, "The idea is that of longing for something to the point of weakness" (*Psalms*, 563–64). The psalmist is weeping and waiting for the Lord to deliver him from his prideful, arrogant oppressors. He is hurting and in pain, perhaps even at the point of despair. Yet he knows he has a promise, a promise he calls a "righteous promise" or "your righteous oracle" (ibid., 564). God has promised to be there for his people, pledging never to leave or abandon them (Deut 31:6,8; Josh 1:5; Matt 28:20). This is a promise we can always count on. Others may fail us, but our Master never will.

Ask God to Teach You (119:124)

The psalmist has done the right thing (v. 121), called on God to do him good (v. 122), and kept his Word (v. 123). Now he requests God to deal with him based on the intimate covenant relationship, the "faithful love" (Hb *chesed*) he has with the Lord. The psalmist knows from history, Scripture, and experience "that God is not an indifferent, unconcerned deity. He is a loving God; that is why he has given us the Bible" (Boice, *Living*, 121). And because he loves us and has given us his Word, we can boldly and confidently ask him to be our Teacher, to "teach me your statutes."

All of us learn from someone. Wisdom would lead us to seek out the instruction of those who are wisest and who love us the most. What a blessed privilege it is for the Christian to find the wisest and most loving Teacher in the same Master, the Lord Jesus!

God's Servants Ask for Spiritual Insight and Plead with God to Act

PSALM 119:125-126

A servant who loves his master wants to think like his master. He wants to see life as his master sees life. In other words, he wants his master's thoughts to become his thoughts. The disciple of Jesus has an advantage because our Master has revealed his mind in the Bible. We do not have to guess or wonder what he thinks. We simply go to the Holy Scriptures and find the mind of Christ (Phil 2:5). In the Scriptures we discover what honors and pleases him. We also discover what dishonors and displeases him. Verses 125-126 inform us what prayers honor the Lord.

Ask the Lord for Understanding of His Word (119:125)

In verse 125 the psalmist asks for "understanding" so that he may "know" the Word of God, what he calls the Lord's "decrees." His teachable spirit is evident. Alec Motyer comments,

> The three verbs ("teach . . . [understanding] . . . know") form a progression: the divine teacher accompanies his teaching with inspiration, the gift of "discernment" [or "understanding"]. The resultant state is "knowledge," truth grasped. (*Psalms*, 356)

To "know" God's decrees is not merely theoretical or cerebral. It is a knowledge of the heart and soul, a knowledge grasped, loved, and obeyed. Teaching leads to understanding, which leads to experiential knowledge that causes living out what we know and believe. Spurgeon summarizes the idea beautifully:

> The servant of God longs to know in an understanding manner all that the Lord reveals of man and to man; he wishes to be so instructed that he may apprehend and comprehend that which is taught him. A servant should not be ignorant concerning his master, or his master's business; he should study the mind, will, purpose, and aim of him whom he serves, for so only can he complete his service; and as no man knows these things so well as his master himself, he should often go to him for instructions, lest his very zeal should only serve to make him the greater blunderer. (*Treasury*, 369)

Ask the Lord to Vindicate His Reputation (119:126)

The servant of Jesus cares more for the Lord's reputation than his own. He grieves when others "have violated [the LORD's] instruction" ("your law has been broken" ESV). He weeps when people do not honor and obey the instruction of God (v. 136). With amazing boldness and confidence, the psalmist says it is time for God to do something because of the total disregard evil persons have for the Word of God. "Lord," he cries out, "it is time to act." The Lord's name is profaned. His commands are mocked and disregarded. So the psalmist wants God to deal justly and rightly with those who hate him and with those who love him (v. 121). The psalmist longs for deliverance from oppression, but he also longs to see the Lord honored. He pleads, "Bring judgment! Bring revival! Bring both! Do something, Lord, and do it now!"

God's Servants Love the Lord's Word and Hate All That Is False

PSALM 119:127-128

A right knowledge of God's Word will lead us in one of two directions. Either we will love his Word and value it more than anything else, or we will hate it and scorn it, treating it with utter contempt. Servants of Jesus will love it and value it because they recognize it for what it is, the words of God. Servants of the devil, "the father of lies" (John 8:44), will hate it and scorn it because they have been deceived to view the Bible incorrectly. One might say they do not hate Scripture; they simply have no feelings at all toward it. Their disregard, however, amounts to hate because they sadly believe that what it teaches enslaves us. They believe it confines, restricts, suppresses, and limits our potential and possibilities. And they scoff at the notion of being told what to do. The truth that softens the heart of a repentant sinner only hardens the heart of the stubborn.

Affirm the Value of God's Word (119:127)

Verses 127 and 128 begin with the word *therefore* in the ESV, connecting these verses with verses 125-126. Because the psalmist understands and knows his Word intimately, he says, "I love your commands more than gold, even the purest gold" (cf. v. 72). According to Psalm 19:10, the Word of God is "more desirable than gold—than an abundance of pure gold." The psalmist has a passion for the Word. Having gained it as his own through knowledge and understanding, he loves it more than anything the world has to offer. The rich are not those who have much silver and gold. The rich are those who have the Word of God! God's Word is more enriching than gold, more comforting than wealth, and more precious than any earthly treasure. Love it even when you fail to obey it. In time it will bring you to repentance and take you back to where you belong.

Affirm the Truth of God's Word (119:128)

Verse 127 speaks of a holy obsession, while verse 128 speaks of a holy opposition. Verses 127-128 form what could be called "the preacher's confession." These verses speak to his love for the Word, and he proclaims his confidence in the Word he proclaims. In verse 127 he says that he loves the Lord's Word, and in verse 128 he considers all God's Word to be right (ESV).[3] Note the use of the word *all*. He loves all the Lord's Word, and he believes all his words to be true. It is not partially true or even mostly true. All of it, every single word, is right, correct, true, infallible, and inerrant. And because he considers all the Lord's Word to be right, he says, "[I] hate every false way." He hates anything that denies or contradicts the Lord's Word. Christians can and should apply this truth today. God's Word says Jesus is the only Savior (John 14:6), so we ought to hate the lies of universalism and inclusivism. His Word says salvation is by grace through faith (Eph 2:8-9), so we ought to hate works-salvation theologies. His Word says God is both holy and loving (Isa 6:3; 1 John 4:7-8), so we ought to hate the lie that says he is one but not the other. If we love the Lord and his Word, we will also hate Satan and his lies.

Conclusion

Jesus is the quintessential "Servant of the Lord" (see Isa 52:13–53:12). He was consumed with a passion to serve his Father and do his will. This desire is evident from three passages in the Gospel of John:

> *My food is to do the will of him who sent me and to finish his work.* (John 4:34)
>
> *I can do nothing on my own . . . because I do not seek my own will, but the will of him* [the Father] *who sent me.* (John 5:30)
>
> *For I have come down from heaven, not to do my own will, but the will of him who sent me.* (John 6:38)

Jesus teaches us that "a servant is not greater than his master" (John 13:16; 15:20). If our Master, the Lord Jesus, was consumed with a passion to serve his Father and to do his will, can it be any different with us? As Spurgeon says, "We who rejoice that we are sons of God are by no means the less delighted to be his servants" (*Treasury*, 369).

---

[3] The CSB translates verse 128 as "I carefully follow all your precepts." The ESV states a fact while the CSB emphasizes the result.

Reflect and Discuss

1. What does it mean to think more about God than about yourself?
2. How can Christians act as if God exists to serve them? What examples of this are present in your own life?
3. How will you pray differently if you believe that you exist to serve God instead of believing that God exists to serve you?
4. The psalmist reflects on his obedience as he requests God to act. Does God require obedience for him to answer prayers? Why or why not?
5. How should practical wisdom and teaching from Scripture relate to one another?
6. Should learning God's Word be done alone or with others? Why?
7. Why should God's people care whether other people violate his instruction?
8. What does it mean for God to deal with his servants based on his "faithful love" (v. 124)?
9. What can you do to help you not take God's Word for granted?
10. This stanza teaches to love God's Word even when you fail to obey it because "in time it will bring you to repentance and take you back to where you belong." How can our sin make us believe that we should not love God's Word any longer?

Do You Weep over Sin?

PSALM 119:129-136

Main Idea: Pursue a passionate, grace-dependent, Word-centered desire to see God's will accomplished.

I. Do You Have a Passion for the Word of God (119:129-131)?
- A. God's Word is wonderful (119:129).
- B. God's Word gives light (119:130).
- C. God's Word leaves you insatiable (119:131).

II. Do You Seek God's Favor so that You May Honor Him (119:132-135)?
- A. Ask God to be gracious to you (119:132).
- B. Ask God to protect you from sin (119:133).
- C. Ask God to deliver you from your enemies (119:134).
- D. Ask God to bless you with his presence (119:135a).
- E. Ask God to be your teacher (119:135b).

III. Do You Grieve when People Disobey Our Lord's Word (119:136)?
- A. There is a reaction: tears of grief (119:136a).
- B. There is a reason: disregard of the Word of God (119:136b).

Many things in our broken world can bring us to tears. Serious issues like divorce, miscarriages, wayward children, and death make us weep. Even less serious events like romantic breakups, songs, and movies can grip our hearts and cause tears. You may be thinking right now of something or someone who brought you to tears. But have you ever asked yourself, "When was the last time I wept over sin? When was the last time tears streamed down my face because my God was being dishonored and disrespected?" Our answers to these questions are important because they help reveal our passions—what we value and love. Many things in this world vie for our love, but the seventeenth stanza of Psalm 119 shows us what God says Christians should be most passionate about. It does this by prompting us to ask ourselves three questions.

Do You Have a Passion for the Word of God?

PSALM 119:129-131

Psalm 119 is the "Word of God" psalm. Its twenty-two stanzas and 176 verses exalt the beauty, truth, value, and wonder of this magnificent gift from our God. Our God is not silent. He is a talking God, and he talks to us in and through his Word so that we might know him and love him. Our God longs to have a relationship with us. Do we desire to have a relationship with him? If we do, we will make three confessions concerning his Word.

God's Word Is Wonderful (119:129)

The psalmist begins stanza *Pe* (פ) by declaring to God, "Your decrees are wondrous." They are extraordinary and magnificent. Nothing is like his Word. It is a wonder to behold, cherish, and possess. This supernatural, "out of this world" (Motyer, *Psalms*, 356) Word demands a clear response: "Therefore I [Hb *nephesh*] obey them." Something this wonderful must be loved and obeyed, valued, and honored. Jesus is the "Wonderful Counselor" (Isa 9:6). We find his wonderful counsel in his Word.

God's Word Gives Light (119:130)

One of the reasons God's Word is wonderful is that it "brings light." Its unfolding illuminates our soul and "gives understanding to the inexperienced ["simple" ESV]." Willem VanGemeren says that when the door is opened to God's Word, "even those inexperienced in the realities of life ('the simple'; cf. 116:6; Prov 1:4; 14:15) may gain wisdom ('understanding': cf. 19:7)" (*Psalms*, 883). Open the door of God's Word, and light will shine into our lives to guide us to think and to live wisely.

God's Word Leaves You Insatiable (119:131)

Insatiable is not a word we use often. However, it is the right word to capture the thrust of verse 131. It refers to a desire that is impossible to fully satisfy. This constant hunger is exactly what the songwriter had for the Word of God. He opens his mouth and pants. He wants more and more. He cannot get enough. His appetite for the Holy Scriptures cannot be satisfied. Psalm 42:1-2 complements the psalmist's longing in this verse: "As a deer longs for flowing streams, so I long for you, God. I thirst for God, the living God. When can I come and appear before God?" Because he pants for the living God, he pants and longs for his

Word, his commands. Martin Luther says the psalmist opens his mouth "to be taught rather than to teach," so Luther paraphrases the verse, "I have opened my mouth, that I might not want to offer what is mine, but desire to receive what is Yours" (*Psalm 76–126*, 500). We do not long to hear our voices; we long to hear the Lord's.

Do You Seek God's Favor so that You May Honor Him?

PSALM 119:132-135

Motives are important in life. Why we do what we do is especially important for those who serve King Jesus. When it comes to seeking his favor, his blessings, are you motivated by a desire for your recognition or his? Does your glory or his glory drive you? The psalmist is the Lord's servant (v. 135). His Master's reputation is what matters most. It is from this reality that five prayer requests or petitions emerge in verses 132-135.

Ask God to Be Gracious to You (119:132)

Having received in verses 129-131 the wonderful, illuminating Word that he can never get enough of, the psalmist asks the Lord, "Turn to me and be gracious to me." He knows he can make this request for grace from God because this "is your practice toward those who love your name." He loves who the Lord is and what he does. He values his name, his honor, his reputation. So he is confident in asking for the Lord's attention and grace. Spurgeon says, "If God looks and sees us panting [for him], he will not fail to be merciful to us" (*Treasury*, 379).

Ask God to Protect You from Sin (119:133)

Verse 133 is specific in one of the ways God is gracious to his children. It is expressed in a twofold request. First, the psalmist asks, "Make my steps steady through your promise." The idea is that "God should make his life safe and secure . . . fixed and firm" (Ross, *Psalms*, 568–69). Second, and closely related, he says to the Lord, "Don't let any sin dominate me." Sin will try to gain control of us and get us walking down the wrong path. But we must long to honor the Lord. We ask him to protect us from any and all sin so that we may succeed.

Ask God to Deliver You from Your Enemies (119:134)

Once more the oppressors appear (cf. vv. 121-122). Being the Lord's servant does not come without opposition and persecution. The psalmist asks for the Lord's deliverance. He asks God to set him free from those who would take him down and cause him to dishonor the name of his Lord. He asks God to set him free to obey and then says, "I will keep your precepts." Sin and sinners want to defeat us. We need a redeemer to rescue us from them and, as the grand redemptive story teaches, from ourselves.

Ask God to Bless You with His Presence (119:135a)

James Boice comments that the first part of verse 135 "is a conscious echo of the Old Testament benediction, known as the Aaronic blessing" (*Living*, 132). We read in Numbers 6:24-26,

> *May the LORD bless you and protect you; may the LORD make his face shine on you and be gracious to you; may the LORD look with favor on you and give you peace.*

Like Moses, the psalmist asks to see the face of God in his life, to experience his presence and enjoy his favor. He is the Lord's servant. The Lord is his Master. He longs only for the presence and blessing of this one and no other.

Ask God to Be Your Teacher (119:135b)

The Lord is our Master. And because he is our Master, he is also our Teacher. Although God blesses his people with spiritually gifted teachers (Rom 12:7), he is the master Teacher who instructs us concerning his decrees, his words, his commands, his promises, his precepts, his statutes, his judgments, and his instruction. Alec Motyer beautifully ties the two truths of verse 135 together: "The shining face is the teaching of truth. Yahweh's face shines (with delight and favor) as he teaches his truth" (*Psalms*, 357).

Do You Grieve When People Disobey Our Lord's Word?
PSALM 119:136

The psalmist knows the world he lives in well—its brokenness, its pain, its sorrow, and its sin. One would have to be blind not to see it. And it breaks his heart. The final verse of stanza *Pe* reveals the songwriter's reaction to this world, a world that is beaten down and battered. It also reveals why our world groans and hurts so much: sin.

There Is a Reaction: Tears of Grief (119:136a)

The psalmist uses a beautiful word picture to describe his grief. "My eyes pour out streams of tears," he cries. Rivers of water run down his eyes when he sees people, human beings who bear the divine image, disregard the Lord's Word and pay God no mind. Alec Motyer writes, "The context is that Yahweh's revealed truth is so 'wonderful' [v. 129] that it is heart-breaking that anyone should fail to keep it" (*Psalms*, 357). Yet people do not keep God's Word. They prefer the false way rather than the true way (v. 128). They choose to let sin, instead of God's Word, rule their lives (v. 133). The situation is tragic. The child of God should break down and weep.

There Is a Reason: Disregard of the Word of God (119:136b)

The precise cause for the tears is given as this stanza comes to an end: "People do not follow your instruction." The teachings of our Lord that are found in his Word are disobeyed and rejected. They are not valued, so they are discarded as worthless. God gives us his divinely inspired Word, and humanity responds, "We couldn't care less." This is not how those who love God respond. As Spurgeon says, "Spiritual men feel a holy fear of the Lord himself, and most of all lament when they see dishonour cast upon his holy name" (*Treasury*, 380).

Conclusion

Just as sin and the sorrows of this world brought tears to the psalmist, they brought tears to the eyes of the Lord Jesus. John 11:35 reminds us that "Jesus wept." He wept over the death of his dear friend Lazarus. He wept over the sin, sickness, and sorrow of this fallen world. So much grief, so much chaos, so much pain and hurt, so much unbelief. In Luke 19:41 we see our Lord weeping over the city of Jerusalem because of her sin and unbelief. Sin breaks the heart of God. Sin brings tears to the eyes of God. Is the same true for you? Tears over sin demand that we do something. It moved Jesus to go to the cross so that he could turn tears of sorrow into tears of joy.

Reflect and Discuss

1. Why should someone be passionate about God's Word?
2. Can you obey God's Word without being passionate about God's Word? Why or why not?

3. What type of understanding does God's Word give? Describe a time when God's Word gave you understanding to make a decision.
4. What is the psalmist asking for when he asks God to be gracious toward him?
5. Is asking God to protect you from sin a regular pattern in your life? Why or why not? How could this request help you?
6. How does God bless you with his presence if he does not appear physically?
7. What part does God's presence have in the grand redemptive story of the Bible?
8. What does it mean for God to be your Teacher?
9. Why should the sin of others cause you tears? What does the sin of others most commonly cause you to feel?
10. What should Christians desire God to do to those who do not follow his instructions?

Our Righteous God and His Righteous Word

PSALM 119:137-144

Main Idea: The perfect and eternally righteous Word of God should compel us toward love, faith, and trust.

I. Our Righteous God's Word Is Righteous and Faithful (119:137-138).
- A. He is righteous in who he is (119:137a).
- B. He is righteous in what he says (119:137b-138).

II. Our Righteous God's Word Is to Be Obeyed (119:139-141).
- A. Be passionate for God's Word (119:139).
- B. Love God's Word (119:140).
- C. Faithfully recall God's Word (119:141).

III. Our Righteous God's Word Will Endure Forever (119:142-144).
- A. Believe God's Word is righteous and true (119:142).
- B. Delight in God's Word at all times (119:143).
- C. Find life in God's Word through prayer (119:144).

When Christians study the doctrine of God, one of the important categories we investigate is his attributes. As Timothy George well says,

> When theologians ask, "What is God like?" they talk about the divine attributes. God's attributes are also known as his perfections, properties, virtues, and predicates. The attributes characterize God's nature and character. ("The Nature of God," 190)

George goes on to note that

> the attributes of God are too numerous to list; but they include infinity, incomprehensibility, immutability, omnipresence, omniscience, omnipotence, simplicity, eternity, spirituality, holiness, truth, wisdom, goodness, love, righteousness, unity, immensity, fidelity, mercy, self-sufficiency, indivisibility, immeasurability, personality, congruence, glory, blessedness, and freedom. (Ibid.)

Stanza *Tsade* (צ), Psalm 119:137-144, zeros in on one of these divine attributes: righteousness.

A form of the word *righteousness* occurs six times in these eight verses, which is not surprising since each verse begins with the Hebrew letter *Tsade* (צ) and the Hebrew word for "righteous" is *tsedeq* (צדק). Wayne Grudem provides a helpful and simple definition of *righteousness* when he writes, "God's righteousness means that God always acts in accordance with what is right and is himself the final standard of what is right" (*Systematic Theology*, 203). The psalmist will look at this wonderful attribute of our God in three movements. He devotes attention to our righteous God and his righteous Word. This stanza takes the form of a confession. There is only one prayer request, and it comes at the end in verse 144. We should make the psalmist's confession and prayer our own.

Our Righteous God's Word Is Righteous and Faithful
PSALM 119:137-138

Righteousness is not a popular idea in twenty-first-century Western culture. Because it is not a popular idea, most persons have little or no understanding of what righteousness is. Even when people talk about "righteousness," their definitions of righteousness can also differ. So where should we turn to understand what true righteousness is? James Boice is correct when he answers, "Anyone who cares about righteousness and wants to act righteously should study the Bible" (*Living*, 134). Psalm 119:137-144 is an excellent place to start.

He Is Righteous in Who He Is (119:137a)

The psalmist begins this stanza with a straightforward affirmation about our God: "You are righteous, Lord" (*Yahweh*). Your character and nature are characterized by what is right. The apostle Paul tells us the "righteousness of God is revealed" in the gospel (Rom 1:16-17). The apostle John adds that when we sin, "we have an advocate with the Father—Jesus Christ the righteous one" (1 John 2:1). Righteousness is an essential attribute of our great God. Moses writes of God in Deuteronomy 32:4, "All his ways are just. A faithful God, without bias, he is righteous and true."

Our God is the standard of righteousness. No correct understanding of righteousness can be gained outside of him or apart from him.

The Lord alone is righteous. He is the final standard. He is the only standard. If you want to know what righteousness is, then get to know the one true and living God. And if you want to see perfect righteousness in action, then just look at Jesus!

He Is Righteous in What He Says (119:137b-138)

Because the Christian God is righteous in who he is, he is also righteous in what he reveals in his Word. His "judgments are just" (v. 137b). There are no lies. There is no deception. "The decrees you issue are righteous" (v. 138), as the psalmist says. He reinforces this truth by saying that God's decrees are "altogether trustworthy." Righteousness and faithfulness characterize the Word of God. God's righteous revelation is the natural expression of his absolute and perfect righteousness. God's Word is altogether true and trustworthy because he inspired it (2 Tim 3:16). Therefore, to doubt and question the righteous nature of God's Word is to question the righteous nature of God himself. The two are intertwined.

Our Righteous God's Word Is to Be Obeyed

PSALM 119:139-141

Our righteous God did not give us his righteous and trustworthy Word for us merely to contemplate and reflect on it, as important as both are. He gave us his Word for us to passionately pursue him and obey his Word. Concerning God's words, Spurgeon writes, "It is not left to our choice whether we will accept them or no; they are issued by royal command, and are not to be questioned" (*Treasury*, 390). That which is not to be questioned is to be obeyed without question. The psalmist develops the idea of obedience in three helpful ways.

Be Passionate for God's Word (119:139)

The psalmist testifies to his passion for God's Word with a negative example: "My anger ["zeal" ESV, NIV, NASB] overwhelms me because my foes forget your words." Zeal speaks of a

> passionate intensity over things that matter. . . . Here it is zeal to defend God's Word because the enemies have forgotten it, meaning they have not paid attention to its revelation or regulations. (Ross, *Psalms*, 572)

The psalmist grieves with anguish in his soul over the reality that those who oppose him care nothing for God's Word. It does not matter to them. But the psalmist cannot stand idly like a passive observer; that is not an option. It would trouble him that people disregard God's Word and take the lives of the unborn. It would trouble him that people disregard God's Word and practice bigotry and racism. It would trouble him that people disregard God's Word and neglect the poor and the immigrant. It would trouble him that people disregard God's Word and even mock the Lord Jesus, the Savior of the world. The psalmist is passionate about these things. We should be passionate about them as well.

Love God's Word (119:140)

The trustworthiness of God's Word is something the psalmist knows well from experience. God's Word can be described as "well tried" (ESV) and "completely pure" (CSB). This purity means that God's Word has been discovered "to be pure, like gold that has been refined" (Ross, *Psalms*, 573). Therefore, the psalmist's response makes perfect sense: "Your servant loves it." The servant of the Lord loves the Word of God and the God of the Word. His heart and soul are joined to the Word of God like one lover is joined to another! And because he loves the Word, he is passionate about it (v. 139), he will not forget it (v. 141), it is his delight (v. 143), and he will live by it (v. 144). Jesus said it well in Matthew 4:4: "Man must not live on bread alone, but on every word that comes from the mouth of God." Scripture must be our life. Scripture must be our love.

Faithfully Recall God's Word (119:141)

In the eyes of the world, the one who loves and lives by the Word of God is a fool. The psalmist says he is "insignificant and despised." Because he loves God and his Word with all his heart, his enemies mock him and make fun of him. Still, he says, "I do not forget your precepts." He remains faithful to the Lord's Word and true to him no matter what. He loves him and his Word more than the opinions of people. As Paul says in Galatians 1:10, "Am I striving to please people? If I were still trying to please people, I would not be a servant of Christ." When we are ridiculed by this world, we should faithfully recall the Lord's Word. We must commit to obey it and not forget it.

Our Righteous God's Word Will Endure Forever

PSALM 119:142-144

Things in this broken and fallen world do not last. Things wear out. Things break and cannot be repaired. We will all grow old and die, becoming in this world nothing more than a memory. Thankfully, there is something that will never wear out, become obsolete, or fade away. It is the righteous character of our eternal God and his righteous Word. The prophet Isaiah got it exactly right: "The grass withers, the flowers fade, but the [righteous] word of our [righteous] God remains forever" (Isa 40:8)

Believe God's Word Is Righteous and True (119:142)

Once again, the psalmist passionately declares and confesses, "Your righteousness is an everlasting righteousness." God does not change. Therefore, his righteous character will never change; it will last forever. It will remain an everlasting righteousness. And because God is everlastingly and eternally righteous, his "instruction is true." This is such an important and encouraging truth. Politicians lie. CEOs lie. Employees lie. Spouses lie. Parents lie. Children lie. Even Christians lie. But our God never, ever lies. Never! He is righteous, and his Word is righteous. He is true, and his Word is true. Concerning the Scriptures, Spurgeon is spot on: "We may not say of them that they contain the truth, but that they are the truth" (*Treasury*, 391).

Delight in God's Word at All Times (119:143)

Verse 143 now describes the activity of the foes from verse 139. They inflict on the psalmist "trouble and distress." His troubles have brought him emotional distress and "anguish" (ESV). They have "overtaken" him (CSB), "found [him] out" (ESV). Like hounds after their prey, they have tracked him down. He is discouraged and almost overwhelmed by their relentless attacks. But God has rescued him by his Word. Taking his focus off his enemies, he has fled to the Word of God, which is his "delight." Brought low by his oppressors (vv. 121,134), he is lifted up and given renewed vigor (v. 144) by the commands of the Lord. Delighting in the Word of God no matter what may come his way, he is strengthened and empowered to press on and stay in the fight.

Find Life in God's Word through Prayer (119:144)

This is the only prayer request in stanza *Tsade,* and it is a prayer for understanding. It is preceded by a second declaration that the Lord and his "decrees are righteous forever" (cf. v. 142). God is righteous forever, and his Word is righteous forever. The psalmist longs to understand the righteous Word of his righteous God to the end so "that I may live" (ESV). *The Message* paraphrases verse 144 very well: "The way you tell me to live is always right; help me understand it so I can live life to the fullest."

Conclusion

"Life's adversities should drive us all the more to our Bibles" (Motyer, *Psalms,* 357). That is certainly true for the Christian. It was certainly true of the Lord Jesus. When Satan confronted and tempted Christ in the wilderness, each and every time he went to the righteous Word of his righteous Father and defeated his foe (Matt 4:1-11). Zeal for the Word of God consumed our Savior (v. 139). Despised and treated as nothing by this world, he did not forget the words of Holy Scripture (v. 141). Trouble and anguish dogged him all the way to Golgotha, but he continually delighted in the commands of the Bible (v. 143). He knew his Father's Word was both righteous and faithful (v. 138) and that eternal life was on the other side of the cross and the empty tomb! This is how our Lord lived. This is how those of us who follow him should live as well. Delight in his Word. There is life—abundant life—for all who do.

Reflect and Discuss

1. Why is it important that both God and his Word are righteous? What would it change if either were not righteous?
2. What are some similarities and differences between the ways the Bible and your culture define righteousness?
3. How does one's definition of righteousness affect how one thinks and lives?
4. Based on this stanza's teaching of righteousness, how would you define unrighteousness?
5. Are the Bible and your culture ever at odds with what they define as unrighteous? If so, how?
6. How can Christians speak in such a way that they proclaim and promote biblical righteousness but not act self-righteously?

7. Is righteousness an inward character trait or an outward action?
8. Does pursuing biblical righteousness ever come at a cost?
9. What is the reward of pursuing biblical righteousness?
10. How does one attain the perfect righteousness that Jesus has?

I Will Never Leave You or Abandon You

PSALM 119:145-152

Main Idea: Those who are far from the Lord will persecute God's people, but God is near to his people and hears them.

I. Call on the Lord in Prayer in Full Confidence that He Will Answer You (119:145-149).
   A. Call on the Lord with your whole heart (119:145).
   B. Call on the Lord to deliver you (119:146).
   C. Call on the Lord early in the morning (119:147-148).
   D. Call on the Lord knowing he loves you (119:149a).
   E. Call on the Lord because he is just and gives us life (119:149b).

II. Remember that Evil People Disregard the Word of God and Will Come after You (119:150).
   A. Evil people will pursue us and try to take us down (119:150a).
   B. Evil people care nothing for the instruction of God (119:150b).

III. Never Forget that the Lord Is Always Near and His Word Endures Forever (119:151-152).
   A. The Lord is always with us (119:151a).
   B. The Lord's Word is true (119:151b).
   C. The Lord's Word will last forever (119:152).

When Paul was imprisoned for the second time and faced imminent execution, he wrote a deeply personal letter to his young "son" in the ministry. That letter is 2 Timothy. At the end of the letter, the aged apostle speaks honestly about both his sorrow and his comfort. He writes in 2 Timothy 4:16-17,

> *At my first defense, no one stood by me, but everyone deserted me. May it not be counted against them. But the Lord stood with me and strengthened me, so that I might fully preach the word and all the Gentiles might hear it. So I was rescued from the lion's mouth.*

All deserted him, but not the Lord. The Father stood with him and strengthened him. He kept the promise we find in Hebrews 13:5: "I will never leave you or abandon you" (cf. Deut 31:6,8; Josh 1:5).

Stanza *Qoph* (ק), Psalm 119:145-152, resonates with Paul's confidence and hope. When our enemies draw near, we can rest assured that our Lord is even nearer. He knows where we are, and he knows what we are going through. As Psalm 46:1 promises, "God is our refuge and strength, a helper who is always found in times of trouble." Three movements guide us through this song of blessed assurance.

Call on the Lord in Prayer in Full Confidence that He Will Answer You

PSALM 119:145-149

This stanza begins with the psalmist sharing his prayer habits coupled with a prayer request. He is surrounded by enemies who would ruin him if they could, but the promises and presence of his Lord are all the assurance he needs to persevere and prevail. As he discusses his prayer pattern, he highlights five characteristics of his prayer life—characteristics that should be true of our prayer life as well.

Call on the Lord with Your Whole Heart (119:145)

Fervent, passionate prayer should be evident in our prayer life. The psalmist declares, "I call with all my heart." With all that he is, with every fiber of his being, he asks his Lord to "answer." The genuineness and earnestness of his prayer are affirmed in his pledge: "I will obey your statutes." James Boice writes, "Prayer should be deeply earnest. The psalmist's prayers were, and it is this that drove him to God's Word" (*Living*, 138). A passion for prayer and a passion for the Word of God should always go together. They should be inseparable twins in our life.

Call on the Lord to Deliver You (119:146)

A prayer for salvation from his enemies follows the psalmist's cry for answered prayer: "I call to you; save me, and I will keep your decrees." Verse 146 restates and reinforces verse 145. Willem VanGemeren helpfully puts the two verses together: "[The psalmist] feverishly presents his lament before the Lord so that God may 'answer' (v. 145; cf. v. 26) him by delivering him from adversity ('save me')" (*Psalms*, 885). Again, his request has warrant. "I will obey your statutes. . . . And I will keep your decrees." Trust and obedience, prayer and obedience, are a God honoring combination for receiving answers to our prayers.

Call on the Lord Early in the Morning (119:147-148)

Verse 145 speaks to the passion for prayer. Verses 147-148 reveal the psalmist's pattern of prayer: "I rise before dawn and cry out for help. . . . I am awake through each watch of the night." He prays early in the morning. When he awakens throughout the night, he turns to his Lord in prayer. First thing in the morning, even before the sun rises, he cries out to him in prayer. He cries for help because of the evil men who are after him (v. 150). He cries out in "hope," and he "meditate[s] on your promise." Early prayers and early meditations on the Word are another powerful prayer combination.

Call on the Lord Knowing He Loves You (119:149a)

The psalmist will pray and obey. He will pray early and meditate throughout the night on God's Word. He will also pray confidently because of the Lord's *chesed*, his "faithful love." The psalmist's request, "Hear my voice," in verse 149 complements the request, "Answer me," in verse 145. He prays audibly. The confidence of his cry is founded on the Lord's loyal love, the Lord's faithful covenant love for those who belong to him. We can come to our Lord anytime and anywhere, confident he hears us. Why? Because we know he loves us as a father loves his children. His love is a true, tender, genuine, and affectionate love that we do not have to doubt. He has told us he loves us. He always keeps his word. Nothing more needs to be said.

Call on the Lord because He Is Just and Gives Us Life (119:149b)

The prayer of verse 149 anticipates the dire situation of verse 150. Evil persecutors are closing in around the psalmist. Their intentions are evil and unjust. He appeals to the Lord ("give me life") on the basis of God's justice. He needs his God to deliver him from his enemies because he cannot deliver himself. They are too numerous and powerful for him, but they are not too many or too strong for the Lord. "LORD" (vv. 145,149,151), he cries, "give me life, or I die. Draw near to me, or I perish. I know you love me. I know you will not fail me. You are near, just, and loving. You are all I need."

Remember that Evil People Disregard the Word of God and Will Come after You

PSALM 119:150

The psalmist cries for help in verse 147. He asks God to preserve his life in verse 149. Verse 150 now provides the reason for his requests. Once again, he is being tracked down by oppressors (vv. 121,122,134) and foes (v. 139), whom he now describes as "those who pursue evil plans," those "who persecute me with evil purpose" (ESV).

Evil People Will Pursue Us and Try to Take Us Down (119:150a)

The Message describes the evil men of verse 150 as "those out to get me." Enemies of the songwriter have appeared throughout Psalm 119, and now they are closing in on him with nothing but evil intentions. One gets the sense that they are determined and relentless. They will not stop until they have captured and destroyed this man (or woman) of God. Christians have endured persecution throughout redemptive history. We should never forget that our Lord Jesus experienced persecution too. We should not be surprised when it is our experience as well (John 15:20; 1 Pet 4:12-13)

Evil People Care Nothing for the Instruction of God (119:150b)

The psalmist says those who pursue evil plans against him "are far from your instruction." In other words, they hate him because they hate God and his Word. Hate for God's people and hate for God always go together. Jesus addressed this reality at some length in John 15:18-25. The entire section is worth our reflection and meditation in the context of this stanza. There Jesus says,

> *If the world hates you, understand that it hated me before it hated you. If you were of the world, the world would love you as its own. However, because you are not of the world, but I have chosen you out of it, the world hates you. Remember the word I spoke to you: "A servant is not greater than his master." If they persecuted me, they will also persecute you. If they kept my word, they will also keep yours. But they will do all these things to you on account of my name, because they don't know the one who sent me. If I had not come and spoken to them, they would not be guilty of sin. Now they have no excuse for their sin. The one who hates me also hates my Father. If I had not done the works among*

them that no one else has done, they would not be guilty of sin. Now they have seen and hated both me and my Father. But this happened so that the statement written in their law might be fulfilled: They hated me for no reason.

Never Forget that the Lord Is Always Near and His Word Endures Forever

PSALM 119:151-152

In Revelation 21–22 John gives a glorious vision of eternity and the final home for God's children. In Revelation 21:3 a wonderful promise thunders forth from the throne of heaven, from which our God declares, "God's dwelling is with humanity, and he will live with them. They will be his peoples, and *God himself will be with them and will be their God*" (emphasis added). The promised eternal presence of God is indeed a future hope and reality. But it is a present hope and reality as well. Romans 8:38-39 says it so well:

> *For I am persuaded that neither death nor life, nor angels nor rulers, nor things present nor things to come, nor powers, nor height nor depth, nor any other created thing will be able to separate us from the love of God that is in Christ Jesus our Lord.*

The final verses of stanza *Qoph* reaffirm this blessed truth as well.

The Lord Is Always with Us (119:151a)

The persecutors with evil intentions have come near to the psalmist. If he is not careful, their presence can blind him to a far greater presence that is even nearer. He will not allow that to happen, and neither should we. In bold faith we declare no matter what our circumstances may be, "You are near, Lord." Our covenant-keeping God is with us wherever we are and in whatever we are going through. Our enemies may come after us and get very close. They may even persecute us and inflict great evil on us. But do not be distressed or grow fainthearted. The Lord is near, and he is in you by his Spirit! Recall 1 John 4:4: "The one who is in you is greater than the one who is in the world."

The Lord's Word Is True (119:151b)

How do we know the Lord is with us and that he will never leave us or abandon us? We know because God always keeps his word. The songwriter confidently declares, "All your commands are true." All your words are true. Spurgeon puts it like this:

> God neither commands a lie, nor lies in his commands. . . . If all God's commands are truth, then the true man will be glad to keep near to them, and therein he will find the true God near him. . . . God is near and God is true, therefore his people are safe. (*Treasury*, 403)

The Lord's Word Will Last Forever (119:152)

Allen Ross says,

> The testimonies of God may be ancient, founded long ago, but they are not obsolete. . . . [T]he assurance of God's presence with the believer and all that implies is an eternally valid promise. (*Psalms*, 579)

The psalmist closes this stanza with another word of assurance and confidence in the Lord grounded in experience. "Long ago I learned." Your faithfulness is not new news to me. "Long ago I learned from your decrees that you have established them forever." What God said long ago is still true today, and it will be true tomorrow and forever! The hymn "How Firm a Foundation" wonderfully declares, "The soul that on Jesus has leaned for repose; I will not, I will not desert to his foes."

Conclusion

The Christian band Third Day recorded a song titled "Cry Out to Jesus" in 2005 that beautifully complements the hope and promise of stanza *Qoph* in Psalm 119. At every time of day, everywhere you are, and in every circumstance of life, cry out to your Savior. He will listen and be near to you.

Reflect and Discuss

1. Why should Christians be confident when they pray? What passages of Scripture talk about Christians' confidence before God?
2. What does praying "in full confidence" look like?
3. What in the psalmist's prayer is similar to or different from how you normally pray? How do the differences challenge you to pray?
4. After the psalmist asks God to answer his prayer, he says he will obey God. Are you committed to obeying God no matter how he answers your prayers?

5. Why does the psalmist mention the time of his prayer ("before dawn")? Does the time when we pray matter? Why or why not?
6. How does sin affect your prayer life? What does the gospel teach about God's love that should shape how we view prayer when we sin?
7. Should a Christian pray every day? Why or why not? What often prevents you from praying daily?
8. Do you find yourself praying more when life is comfortable or when life is difficult? Why?
9. The psalmist sings that God is near him. Why is this important for him?
10. What role does the nearness of God play in the redemptive story line of Scripture (creation, fall, redemption, restoration)?

Our God Is the Giver of Life

PSALM 119:153-160

Main Idea: Salvation and life come from God, who gives his promises, mercy, and love to those who seek and honor him.

I. Ask the Lord for Life according to His Promise (119:153-155).
- A. Do not forget that the Lord is your advocate (119:153-154).
- B. Do not forget that the wicked are doomed (119:155).

II. Ask the Lord for Life according to His Judgments (119:156-158).
- A. The Lord's mercy is great (119:156).
- B. The number of our enemies is many (119:157-158).

III. Ask the Lord for Life according to His Faithful Love (119:159-160).
- A. God's Word should be loved (119:159).
- B. God's Word is true (119:160a).
- C. God's Word will endure forever (119:160b).

An honest assessment of the Christian life recognizes that there are good days and bad days. There are hills and there are valleys. But we cannot experience the mountaintops without walking through the valleys. And getting to the mountaintop always involves first climbing the mountain. The psalmist has walked many times through the valley of "affliction." He has climbed mountains called "persecutors," "adversaries," and the "faithless" (vv. 157-158 ESV). But along the way he discovered the life that only God can give. He discovered that the Lord faithfully gives life and revives according to his promises, his Word, and his faithful love.

Stanza *Resh* (ר) comprises verses 153-160. Three times we see the prayer, "Give me life according to . . ." (vv. 154,156,159 ESV). The psalmist believes God will plead his cause and redeem his life. Our God is the giver of life, and he is always ready to hear our cries!

Ask the Lord for Life according to His Promise

PSALM 119:153-155

This world can be cruel and difficult. Sometimes the weight of opposition is almost crushing. If God does not rescue us, we will not make it. The psalmist is desperate for divine help. Five imperatives in the first two verses of the stanza convey his desperation. He says, "consider," "rescue," "champion," "redeem," and "give me life." Desperate times demand desperate actions. The laments and petitions of the psalmist are passionate and strong. He is certain that God is on his side and that God will hear his prayer.

Do Not Forget that the Lord Is Your Advocate (119:153-154)

The psalmist asks God to "consider my affliction." He asks the Lord to see his affliction with the hope that God will "rescue me." He needs divine intervention. Further, he needs a divine advocate who will argue on his behalf (cf. 1 John 2:1-2). Using language from the courts and from lawsuits, the psalmist pleads for Yahweh to champion his cause (Ross, *Psalms*, 581). He is confident that God will not only plead his case but also that the Lord will redeem him from his affliction. The Lord will rescue him and, in the process, give him life as the Lord promised (v. 154). God has repeatedly promised in his Word to defend and protect his people if they honor him. The psalmist has not forgotten the instructions of the Lord (v. 153). He has obeyed. In fact, he loves the Word of God (v. 159). He is confident God will deliver and revive his soul just as he has promised.

Do Not Forget that the Wicked Are Doomed (119:155)

Verse 155 contrasts with verses 153-154. The psalmist knows the salvation of the Lord. He knows the Lord's concern, advocacy, redemption, and life. Sadly, "salvation is far from the wicked"; it is nowhere in sight. The actions of the wicked expose their character: "They do not study your statutes." They have no desire for the things of God. The life he offers does not interest them. They disregard his Word. What matters to God does not matter to them. Unlike the psalmist, they forget God's instruction and do not try to learn his statutes. This hardness is the way of the wicked. If they stay on this path, they will never find salvation. If they stay on this path, a terrifying judgment and an eternal hell are their destiny. Those who know the salvation found only in Christ must look to him to save them, "snatching them from the fire" before it is too late (Jude 23).

Ask the Lord for Life according to His Judgments

PSALM 119:156-158

The psalmist has asked the Lord for life, for the Lord to "revive" (NASB) him according to his promise (v. 154). Now he asks the Lord for life and reviving "according to your judgments" or "rules" (ESV). There are positive and negative reasons for his request. He knows that the Lord's "compassions are many" (v. 156). He also knows that his own "persecutors and foes are many" (v. 157). Opposition will not overwhelm him because he knows, "the one who is in [me] is greater than the one who is in the world" (1 John 4:4).

The Lord's Mercy Is Great (119:156)

The Lord's "compassions are many" ("Great is your mercy" ESV). Spurgeon beautifully comments, "Here the psalmist pleads the largeness of God's mercy, the immensity of his tender love . . . mercies many, mercies tender, mercies great" (*Treasury*, 414). Because God is compassionate and looks with favor and kindness on those who are his, the psalmist can boldly ask, "Give me life according to your judgments." The psalmist appeals to God's compassion and character. He knows the Lord's compassions are many, and he knows the Lord's judgments are trustworthy. Why? Because "the entirety of your word is truth" (v. 160).

The Number of Our Enemies Is Many (119:157-158)

Those who love God and seek to obey him need his many mercies. Why? Because the "persecutors and foes" of verse 157 and the "disloyal" ("faithless" ESV) of verse 158 "are many." Opposition is great; it is relentless. Those who do not seek God (v. 155) will never applaud us. They will despise us, mock us, and ridicule us. In the face of such opposition, we must have the resolve of the psalmist in verse 157: "I have not turned from your decrees." The faithless who ignore God and reject his truth should give rise to "disgust" in us (v. 158). Their agenda and goals are not ours. Our love and loyalty to our Lord must be our anchor and must guide our path. Compromise cannot be an option when it comes to our obedience to our God. As Ross eloquently says, "Nothing these people can say or do will make me abandon the path of righteousness laid down in God's Word" (*Psalms*, 583). This obedience is not legalism. It is loyalty to our Lord.

Ask the Lord for Life according to His Faithful Love

PSALM 119:159-160

The Hebrew word *chesed* is one of the most precious and theologically rich words in the Bible. Its many translations in English reflect this richness: "steadfast love," "faithful love," "covenant love," "loyal love," "mercy," and "lovingkindness." The word describes "the faithful and loving care of the covenant God for his people and their faithful love in return to him and other covenant members" (Ross, *Psalms*, 569). It occurs almost 250 times in the Old Testament, and it provides the basis for the psalmist's third plea for life and reviving (vv. 154,156,159). Again, the psalmist asks the Lord to "consider." In verse 153 he asks the Lord to look at his afflictions and difficulties. Now, in verse 159, he asks the Lord to look at his love.

God's Word Should Be Loved (119:159)

The psalmist loves the Word of God. It is his "consuming passion" (Boice, *Living*, 156). And he loves the Word of God because he knows he is loved by the God of the Word. He has experienced the personal love of the covenant-keeping, covenant-loving God. He is loved by God, and he loves God and his Word. With confidence, he asks a third time, "Lord, give me life" (NASB, "Revive me, O Lord"). To love God is to love his Word. It is impossible to do one without the other.

God's Word Is True (119:160a)

When the psalmist writes, "The entirety of your word is truth," he powerfully describes Scripture's complete and total truthfulness. It is difficult to imagine how the psalmist could have said it any stronger. *The Message* paraphrases this verse as, "Your words all add up to the sum total: Truth." Ross says, "The chief characteristic of God's Word is truth. Everything God has said is reliable, because he himself is the truth (see John 14:6)" (*Psalms*, 584). The words *inerrant* and *infallible* capture the psalmist's conviction about the truthfulness of Holy Scripture. God's Word is true and without error in what it teaches.

God's Word Will Endure Forever (119:160b)

Isaiah 40:8 says, "The grass withers, the flowers fade, but the word of our God remains forever." The prophet and the psalmist were of one mind when it came to the enduring nature of the infallible and inerrant Word of God. Not just some—not even merely most—of it is true and enduring. No, "the entirety of your word is truth, each of [the LORD's] righteous judgments endures forever." God is forever. His word is truth. Therefore, God's Word is truth forever. Few things last forever. Most things eventually fail. Praise God that that is not the case with his Word!

Conclusion

Spurgeon says, "The Scriptures are as true in Genesis as in Revelation, and the five books of Moses are as inspired as the four Gospels" (*Treasury*, 416). What is true of the written Word is equally true of the living Word. The incarnate Word, the Lord Jesus Christ, is "full of grace and truth" (John 1:14). He is "the way, the truth, and the life" (John 14:6). God gives life, eternal life, to all who come to him. He has made a promise! He loves you with a steadfast and faithful love! Salvation may be far from those who love wickedness; however, it

> *is near you, in your mouth and in your heart. . . . If you confess with your mouth, "Jesus is Lord," and believe in your heart that God raised him from the dead, you will be saved.* (Rom 10:8-9)

Reflect and Discuss

1. Where does the psalmist gain this confidence to pray during difficulty?
2. How will you react to difficult circumstances if you forget the Lord is your advocate?
3. How does remembering that "salvation is far from the wicked" influence the way the psalmist understands and reacts to his circumstances?
4. What are some of the many ways the Lord has been compassionate to you?
5. What circumstances in your life in addition to "persecutors and foes" could tempt you to turn from God or disregard his Word?
6. Can good circumstances cause you to disregard God and his Word? If so, how?

7. Reread how this commentary describes the word *chesed.* Why must God's people have faithful love with one another in addition to faithful love for him?
8. This stanza argues, "To love God is to love his Word." Why is it impossible to love God without loving his Word?
9. What comparisons and contrasts do you see the psalmist making in these verses? How does this help the psalmist communicate his message?
10. Why does it matter that God's Word "endures forever"?

I Stand Amazed in Your Presence

PSALM 119:161-168

Main Idea: God's people can always respond with love and praise because they have the ultimate treasure—his Word.

I. Expect Unjust Persecution, but Trust the Lord (119:161).
II. Praise the Lord Continually (119:162-164).
III. Enjoy the Peace the Lord Gives to Those Who Love Him (119:165-166).
IV. Keep the Lord's Word with All Your Soul (119:167-168).

In the hymn "I Stand Amazed in the Presence," the first stanza begins,

> I stand amazed in the presence
> Of Jesus the Nazarene,
> And wonder how he could love me,
> A sinner, condemned, unclean.

The chorus beautifully parallels and complements those words:

> How marvelous! How wonderful!
> And my song shall ever be;
> How marvelous! How wonderful!
> Is my Savior's love for me!

That the Lord loves condemned and undeserving sinners is an amazing, marvelous, and wonderful reality. There is only one proper response to this love: to love him in return as we stand in awe of his Word (v. 161) and to praise him throughout the day (v. 164).

Three times in stanza *Sin/Shin* (ש) the psalmist expresses his love for the Lord and his Word (vv. 163,165,167). He would quickly affirm that his love for God and God's instruction flows from the "hope for your salvation" (v. 166). We do not obey God to be accepted; we obey because we are accepted. We do not obey to be loved; we obey because we are loved. First John 4:19 is a fundamental truth that runs from Genesis to Revelation and throughout Psalm 119. John writes, "We love [God and others] because he [God] first loved us." Such love prepares us for the realities of life we must be ready to face—realities that are sometimes painful and stressful.

Expect Unjust Persecution, but Trust the Lord

PSALM 119:161

Opposition and persecution of God's children sometimes originate from high places. Further, the persecution we experience may be unjust and unfair. Verse 161 begins with the psalmist's straightforward recognition of this truth: "Princes have persecuted me without cause." Those in positions of power and leadership have mistreated him, taken advantage of him, and hurt him. There was no justification for what they did. What they did was wrong.

All over the world brothers and sisters in Christ face severe persecution from evil and oppressive governments. They suffer imprisonment, torture, and loss of jobs and homes. Some suffer martyrdom. Some, regrettably, may even suffer persecution in the form of abuse within the church of the Lord Jesus Christ. Men in power exploit the vulnerable through sexual abuse, taking advantage of their positions of power. Rather than serve like shepherds, they ravage like wolves.

The psalmist knows that the hope and cure for such persecution and mistreatment ultimately reside in the heart and the ministry of the Word. He flees to God and his Word. He will not fear his persecutors. With boldness, he declares, "My heart fears only your word." The ESV translates the verse, "My heart stands in awe of your word." These verses mean he will not tremble at his attackers; he will only tremble in awe and respect of his Lord and his Lord's Word. Spurgeon is right when he writes, "We are not likely to be disheartened by persecution, or driven by it into sin, if the word of God continually has supreme power over our minds" (*Treasury*, 423). Evil men will do evil things, but our good God will do good things in the midst of evil (Gen 50:20; Rom 8:28). Flee to him. Fear him. Love him. Trust him. Stand in awe of him. He will be all you need (Phil 4:19).

Praise the Lord Continually

PSALM 119:162-164

When our heart "fears" or "stands in awe of" (ESV) God's Word, certain reactions or responses will be natural. First, we will "rejoice over [God's] promise like one who finds vast treasure" (v. 162). The word "treasure" or "spoil," Motyer says, "points to the fruits of victory" (*Psalms,* 362). The psalmist raises a penetrating question: "Are we meant to take this seriously—that in the constant wear and tear of princely opposition, victory and its rich consequences come to the lover of God's Word?" (ibid.). This is exactly what the psalmist is saying. During persecution, when the Word is doing its work in the heart, we rejoice and celebrate its amazing power like one who has discovered a great treasure.

There is a second response to the work of the Word in our heart: we "hate and abhor falsehood" and "love [the LORD's] instruction" (v. 163). Perhaps the persecution of those in power included lies about the psalmist. How common, unfortunately, this is. People in power lie to further their agenda and get their way. And they often succeed. We can be tempted to follow their actions if we are not careful. The remedy for such temptation is evident: we love the Lord's Word, which is the word of truth (v. 160). As we love his Word, we must hate and abhor falsehood. *Hate* and *abhor* are strong words of rejection. Ross notes *abhor* carries the idea of "loathing and disgust" (*Psalms,* 587). We have already seen this reaction in Psalm 119 (vv. 113,128). We love the truth that flows from the nature and character of our God. In contrast, we hate and loathe every lie and falsehood (cf. John 8:44).

A third response appears in verse 164. "I praise you seven times a day for your righteous judgments." This is a beautiful and poetic way of saying, "I praise you all day long for the righteous character of your words, instructions, judgments." Praise is the songwriter's weapon against his persecutors. Praise for the Lord's Word, which he loves and which fills his heart, is his victory song when others wrong him. He is in awe of the Lord's Word. He rejoices at his Word! He loves his Word. He praises him for his Word. Oh, how great is the Word of God!

Enjoy the Peace the Lord Gives to Those Who Love Him

PSALM 119:165-166

The praise of our lips (v. 164) will lead to peace in our hearts (v. 165) and hope in our souls (v. 166). Because I "love your instruction," great or abundant peace is mine. This truth resembles Philippians 4:6-7:

> *Don't worry about anything, but in everything, through prayer and petition with thanksgiving, present your requests to God. And the peace of God, which surpasses all understanding, will guard your hearts and minds in Christ Jesus.*

Because the songwriter's heart is at peace, "nothing makes [him] stumble." The Lord's Word clears our path so that we can walk safely and securely, even when people persecute us and spread lies about us. We do not retaliate against them because we trust the God whose Word we love. We make good decisions in the right way, at the right time, and for the right reasons because we love and are led by the Word of God.

Peace in our heart and confidence in our walk now gives way to hope for our salvation, hope for our deliverance and rescue. There is a confident expectation that God will come through in the most difficult and painful situations. Proof of this confidence appears at the end of verse 166: "I . . . carry out your commands." Spurgeon says, "Those who place least reliance upon good works are very frequently those who have the most of them" (*Treasury*, 424). Knowing what salvation promises, we can delight in doing what the Word commands. Willem VanGemeren puts it like this: "In anticipation of that great day of 'salvation' . . . the psalmist gives himself to hopeful waiting (Gen 49:18) and to the practice of godliness" (*Psalms*, 888).

Keep the Lord's Word with All Your Soul

PSALM 119:167-168

Verses 167-168 fittingly summarize stanza *Sin/ Shin*. For the third time the psalmist affirms his love for the Word of God (vv. 163,165,167). There is also a twofold concluding pledge to "obey" or "keep" (ESV) God's Word. Living in the abundance of God's *chesed*, his "faithful love" (v. 159), the psalmist declares, "I obey your decrees" (v. 167) and, "I obey your precepts and decrees" (v. 168). Why does he make such a promise to the Lord? The answer is also twofold: he loves the Lord's decrees "greatly" (v. 167, ESV "exceedingly"), and he knows all his ways are before the Lord (v. 168). The psalmist knows "that everything he does and everywhere he goes is fully known to God" (Ross, *Psalms*, 589). Every action, every word, every thought, and every emotion are before the watchful eye of an omnipresent and omniscient God (Job 34:21). And the psalmist is at peace before the Lord because he loves the Lord's Word with all his heart (v. 161) and soul (*nephesh* in v. 167). He rejoices in the Word (v. 162) and obeys the Word (vv. 166,167,168). He hopes in the Lord's salvation and is certain he will experience it to the fullest measure. He is not arrogant but humble as he walks before an awe-inspiring God. Thomas Manton's insights on this verse are worthy of our careful mediation:

> You are in the sight of God, whether you think so or no. . . . What a noble thing it is always to live in the sight of God. . . . The profit is exceedingly great; by conversing with God often, we become like him. (*Psalm 119*, vol. 3, 437)

Conclusion

I remember a song from the time I was a small boy. I loved it from the beginning of my life, and I pray it will be my song until the end. It captures well the heart of this text. It captures well the essence of the Christian life.

> When we walk with the Lord
> In the light of his Word
> What a glory he sheds on our way!
> Let us do his good will;
> He abides with us still,
> And with all who will trust and obey.
> Trust and obey,
> For there's no other way
> To be happy in Jesus,
> But to trust and obey.

Reflect and Discuss

1. What is the difference between obeying because you are accepted by God and obeying to gain acceptance? What are some ways you can assess which type of obedience you are striving for?
2. Should Christians ever oppose abusive leadership—whether those leaders are in the government or in the church? What should Christians do when those in leadership seem to be abusing their power? How can Christians protect the church from abusive leaders?
3. What does it mean to fear God's Word? Why does the psalmist contrast fearing his persecutors and fearing God's Word? How will fearing God's Word help someone during persecution?
4. What promises does God give in Scripture for those who are being persecuted? How can these passages help someone rejoice in their persecution?
5. Do you view God's Word as "vast treasure"? If not, what prevents you from viewing it this way? What makes God's Word so valuable?

6. How should a Christian respond when persecuted? What are some poor responses and some proper responses?
7. This commentary says that "the praise of our lips will lead to peace in our hearts and hope in our souls." How can praise lead to peace and hope?
8. Is hope for God's salvation a hope for God to act in the present or in the future?
9. What is your natural response to unjust treatment? Are you tempted to disobey God's commands in response? How can remembering that your ways are before God encourage you toward more obedience?
10. What does it mean to love God's commands? How are love for God's commands and obedience to his commands related?

A Sheep's Cry to His Shepherd

PSALM 119:169-176

Main Idea: When in need, go to God with prayer and praise.

I. Lord, Please Hear My Prayer (119:169-170).
II. Lord, Please Receive My Praise (119:171-172).
III. Lord, Please Help Me (119:173-175).
IV. Lord, Please Come and Rescue Me (119:176).

The theme of God as the shepherd of his people is one of the richest in the Bible. In Psalm 23 God is the Lord our shepherd. In Ezekiel 34 God promises his people, "I will establish over them one shepherd, my servant David, and he will shepherd them" (v. 23). Micah 5:2-4 continues this theme and informs us this future shepherd will come out of Bethlehem. John 10 reveals to us that Jesus, the Son of God, is the good shepherd who fulfills all these prophetic promises (see also Heb 13:20; 1 Pet 2:25; 5:4; Rev 7:17).

In the twenty-second and final stanza of Psalm 119, stanza *Taw* (ת), the shepherd imagery is subtly but clearly present as the psalmist pours out his heart in prayer to the Lord. He feels like a wandering sheep who has lost his way. His only hope is that the Lord will come after him and rescue him like a loving shepherd (v. 176). This stanza contrasts strikingly to the previous one, stanza *Sin/Shin* (vv. 161-168). In that stanza the psalmist confesses his faithfulness and dedication to God. Here he pleads in prayer for understanding, deliverance, help, and rescue. The psalmist is confident God will hear him. In harmony with the theme of Psalm 119, his cry for deliverance is "according to your word" (v. 169), "according to your promise" (v. 170).

Lord, Please Hear My Prayer

PSALM 119:169-170

The psalmist comes before the Lord (*Yahweh*) with a "cry" and "plea." As Alec Motyer notes, "There is no cocky bursting into his presence" (*Psalms*, 362). What is the nature of his cry and plea? It is twofold. First, the psalmist says, "Give me understanding according to your word" (v. 169). Second, he says, "Rescue me according to your promise" (v. 170). The two ideas are intertwined. As Michael Wilcock helpfully explains,

> I need to know the right things, in the right spirit, at the right time and for the right purposes. . . . I ask that in the way you know is best, you will order my outward circumstance just as you can order my inward thoughts. (*Psalms*, 218)

The psalmist has an intimate and personal relationship with his Lord. He can come near him and pour out his petition. There is boldness ("cry") but also humility ("plea"). Further, he recognizes the need for grace inwardly and outwardly. He needs the Lord to help his understanding, but he also needs the Lord to "rescue" him. We need the Lord to work on our hearts by means of his Word and to help us with the circumstances and situations in which we find ourselves. We need to understand and see things as he does. We also need his intervention. We need him to act on our behalf. Understanding will enable the psalmist, and us, not to take matters into our own hands. We can trust God to help us understand. We can also trust God to make things right. If we act like fools, our enemies will win the day, but if we respond with biblical wisdom they will go down in defeat. Spurgeon wisely wrote, "The Lord in answer to prayer frequently delivers his children by making them wise as serpents as well as harmless as doves" (*Treasury*, 433–34).

Lord, Please Receive My Praise

PSALM 119:171-172

The psalmist's plea now turns to praise. He is confident that his Lord, the shepherd of his soul, will hear and answer his prayer. Verse 171 reads like the praise of the heart, and verse 172 reads like the praise of the mind. The two, in practice, should never be separated.

In verse 171 the psalmist speaks of his abundant praise of God. "'My lips pour out praise' pictures his worship like a gushing spring of water" (Ross, *Psalms*, 592). There is excitement and enthusiasm in his praise as he contemplates that the Lord will "teach me your statutes." He pairs this excitement with his knowledge about God by paralleling verse 171 with verse 172. "Lips" parallels the "tongue"; "praise" parallels "sings"; and "statutes" parallels "promise." With these parallels the psalmist emphasizes the truth that God's commands are righteous. This truth, at least in part, moved him to praise and to sing to the Lord. The God whom he can come before with his pleas and praise is righteous and just in his ways, his will, and his Word. This is a God we can trust to do what is right because he is himself righteous in who he is. Spurgeon once more says it so well: "When a man has so high an opinion of God's commandments it is little wonder that his lips should be ready to extol the ever-glorious One" (*Treasury*, 434).

Lord, Please Help Me

PSALM 119:173-175

Verse 173 renews the psalmist's plea for deliverance. His plea is intensified by his longing for salvation (v. 174) and his use of the phrase "my soul" (ESV, NASB) in verse 175. The psalmist pleas for God's help by asking that his hand "be ready to help me"; he needs the Lord's mighty hand, his powerful hand, to be ready to help him and to do for him what the songwriter cannot do for himself (Ross, *Psalms*, 593). He grounds his plea in his devotion to the Word of God. He asks with confidence because he has chosen to honor and obey God's precepts. The *Message* reads, "Put your hand out and steady me since I've chosen to live by your counsel."

The psalmist does not ask for God's help with a quick, perfunctory prayer; he has a deep desire, as verse 174 describes: "I long for your salvation, Lord." We need the Lord to deliver us from our enemies and from ourselves (v. 176). We need, as James Boice writes,

> [God's] deliverance from sin—from its penalty, power, and presence—from the evil influences and outlook of the world, and perhaps even from the power of the devil. . . . We can do nothing to deliver ourselves. So we need to ask God for salvation, which is what the psalmist does. (*Living*, 166)

He can ask in confidence because "your instruction is my delight."

In verse 175 the palmist couples a request with a commitment: "Let me live" ("Let my soul live" ESV), and my life will be filled with praise (cf. v. 171). And as he lives for the Lord and praises the Lord with all that he is, he says, "May your judgments help me." He needs and depends on the Lord's help (v. 173) and in the Lord's judgments (v. 175). Who God is and what he teaches will save us and sanctify us. John Goldingay puts it like this:

> Our relationship with Yhwh is founded on Yhwh's grace, commitment, and compassion, and in appealing to Yhwh we appeal to who Yhwh is. Yet our relationship also depends on our obedience. . . . I am myself responsible for walking in Yhwh's way, yet I depend on Yhwh's help in doing so. (*Psalms*, 445)

The psalmist gladly admits that he needs his Lord's help to live. We need his presence, and we need his guidance. The Lord is who we need. His Word is what we need.

Lord, Please Come and Rescue Me

PSALM 119:176

In Psalm 23:2-3 David says of the good shepherd, "He lets me lie down in green pastures; he leads me beside quiet waters. He renews my life; he leads me along the right paths for his name's sake." The anonymous psalmist of Psalm 119 resonates with this image of our God. "I wander like a lost sheep," he says. He needs his Lord, like a shepherd, to come get him and to lead him along the right paths. He is wandering like a lost sheep, but he is still the Lord's "servant." He does not forget the Lord's commands. But he cannot find his way home. His Lord must seek him out; the Lord must find him and safely return him home. John Piper notes that "'lost' in Hebrew also means perishing. Sheep will die if not found" ("The Anatomy of Backsliding"). It is significant and wonderful to point out that even though the sheep has lost sight of his shepherd, the shepherd has not lost sight of his sheep. Not only will the great Shepherd go in search of his wayward sheep; the great Shepherd, as the Suffering Servant, will willingly bear the sins of the sheep as their perfect sacrifice (Isa 53:6). What a wonderful Shepherd we have indeed!

Conclusion

The great Reformer Martin Luther has words that provide a fitting commentary on Psalm 119:176. They are also an appropriate conclusion to the whole psalm. What beautiful words of comfort and encouragement they are:

> Therefore at the end of the psalm he [the psalmist] especially calls to mind the divine pity out of the greatness of his wretchedness. For if he strayed like a lion or a wolf, he would not need to be grieved, but because it is a little lamb that goes

astray, it is a wretchedness that needs a shepherd, pasture, watchmen, a sheepfold, and many other household cares, and the straying one lacks all of them. Indeed, what is most wretched of all is that it does not know how to come back on the way but needs to seek it. Thus this verse is extremely emotional and full of tears, for truly we are all thus going astray, so that we must pray to be visited, sought and carried over by the most godly Shepherd, the Lord Jesus Christ, who is God blessed forever. Amen. (*Psalm 76–126*, 534)

Reflect and Discuss

1. What does it look like to pray with both boldness and humility?
2. What type of "understanding" is the psalmist asking for?
3. Why should you pray for "understanding according to [God's] word" in addition to praying for rescue from your situation?
4. Why does the psalmist's troublesome situation not prevent him from praising or singing to God? Who have you seen exemplify praise during difficulty? How does this encourage you?
5. What songs of praise do you know that are helpful when you need help from the Lord?
6. Is it possible to ask for God's help in a superficial manner? If so, how?
7. Is this psalmist trying to bargain with God in verse 175 by committing to praise him for hearing his prayers? What in this psalm can help you answer this question?
8. How does the psalmist's view of himself as a lost sheep and as a servant affect how he approaches God?
9. How does Psalm 23 help us understand this psalm better?
10. Reflect on all you have read about in Psalm 119. What are some of the main themes that have helped you?

WORKS CITED

Adams, Jere V., editor. *Handbook to the Baptist Hymnal.* Nashville: Convention Press, 1992.

Akin, Daniel, and Bill Curtis. "Adrian Rogers: Faithfulness to the Word of God." Pages 485–86 in *A Legacy of Preaching: Enlightenment to the Present Day,* edited by Benjamin K. Forrest, Kevin King, Dwayne Milioni, and Bill Curtis. Volume 2. Grand Rapids: Zondervan Academic, 2018.

Barna Research. "A Biblical Worldview Has a Radical Effect on a Person's Life." *Barna Group,* December 3, 2003. https://www.barna.com/research/a-biblical-worldview-has-a-radical-effect-on-a-persons-life.

Boice, James Montgomery. *Living by the Book: The Joy of Loving and Trusting God's Word.* Grand Rapids: Baker, 1997.

———. *Psalms: An Expositional Commentary. Volume 3: Psalms 107–150.* Grand Rapids: Baker, 2005.

Bullock, C. Hassell. *Encountering the Book of Psalms: A Literary and Theological Introduction.* Grand Rapids: Baker Academic, 2004.

———. *Psalms (Volume 2: Psalms 73–150).* Grand Rapids: Baker, 2017.

Duncan, Ligon. "Not by Bread Alone—Blessed Are Those Who Walk in the Word." *LigonDuncan.Com.* January 6, 2013. http://ligonduncan.com/psalm-119-not-by-bread-alone-blessed-are-those-who-walk-in-the-word-709.

George, Timothy. "The Nature of God: Being, Attributes, and Acts." Pages 176–241 in *A Theology for the Church.* Edited by Daniel L. Akin. Revised edition. Nashville: B&H, 2014.

Goldingay, John. *Psalms 90–150.* Baker Commentary on the Old Testament Wisdom and Psalms. Grand Rapids: Baker Academic, 2008.

The Gospel Coalition. *The New City Catechism: 52 Questions and Answers for Our Hearts and Minds.* Wheaton, IL: Crossway, 2017.

Grudem, Wayne. *Systematic Theology: An Introduction to Biblical Doctrine.* Grand Rapids: Zondervan, 2000.

Keil, C. F., and Franz Delitzsch. *Commentary on the Old Testament: Psalms.* Translated by Francis Bolton. Volume 5. Peabody, MA: Hendrickson, 2006.

Keller, Timothy. *Walking with God through Pain and Suffering.* New York, NY: Dutton, 2013.

Kidner, Derek. *Psalms 73–150.* Tyndale Old Testament Commentaries. Downers Grove, IL: InterVarsity Press, 1973.

Leupold, H. C. *Exposition of the Psalms.* Grand Rapids: Baker, 1979.

Lewis, C. S. *Mere Christianity.* San Francisco, CA: HarperSanFrancisco, 2001.

———. *The Problem of Pain.* San Francisco, CA: HarperOne, 2015.

Luther, Martin. *The Christian in Society.* Edited by Helmut T. Lehmann and James Atkinson. Luther's Works 2. St. Louis, MO: Fortress, 1962.

———. *First Lectures on the Psalms II: Psalm 76–126.* Edited by Hilton C. Oswald. Luther's Works 11. St. Louis, MO: Concordia Publishing House, 1976.

Manton, Thomas. *Psalm 119.* Volume 1. Oxford: Banner of Trust, 1990.

———. *Psalm 119.* Volume 3. Oxford: Banner of Trust, 1990.

Metaxas, Eric. *Amazing Grace: William Wilberforce and the Heroic Campaign to End Slavery.* New York: HarperCollins, 2007.

Motyer, Alec. *Psalms by the Day: A New Devotional Translation.* Fearn, Ross-shire: Christian Focus, 2016.

"Oprah Talks to Graduates about Feelings, Failure and Finding Happiness." *Stanford Report.* June 15, 2008. http://news.stanford.edu/news/2008/june18/como-061808.html.

Phillips, John. *Exploring Psalms.* Grand Rapids: Kregel, 2002.

Piper, John. "The Anatomy of Backsliding." *Desiring God.* July 6, 1987. https://www.desiringgod.org/messages/the-anatomy-of-backsliding.

———. "How to Delight in God's Word." *Desiring God.* March 26, 2012. https://www.desiringgod.org/articles/how-to-delight-in-gods-word.

———. "Open My Eyes That I May See." *Desiring God.* January 4, 1998. https://www.desiringgod.org/messages/open-my-eyes-that-i-may-see.

———. "Thy Word I Have Treasured in My Heart." *Desiring God.* January 5, 1997. https://www.desiringgod.org/messages/thy-word-i-have-treasured-in-my-heart.

Reardon, Patrick Henry. *Christ in the Psalms.* Ben Lommond, CA: Conciliar, 2000.

Records of the International Council on Biblical Inerrancy. October 15, 2019. http://library.dts.edu/Pages/TL/Special/ICBI.shtml. Dallas Theological Seminary.

Rogers, Joyce. *Love Worth Finding: The Life of Adrian Rogers and His Philosophy of Preaching.* Nashville: B&H, 2005.

Ross, Allen P. *A Commentary on the Psalms: 90–150.* Kregel Exegetical Library. Grand Rapids: Kregel, 2014.

Schaeffer, Francis A. *Escape from Reason.* Downers Grove, IL: InterVarsity Press, 2006.

Spurgeon, C. H. *The Treasury of David: Psalms 111–150.* Volume 3. Grand Rapids: Zondervan Pub. House, 1979.

"The Top 50 Books That Have Shaped Evangelicals." *Christianity Today.* October 6, 2006. https://www.christianitytoday.com/ct/2006/october/23.51.html.

VanGemeren, Willem A. *Psalms.* The Expositors Bible Commentary. Edited by Tremper Longman III and David E Garland. Revised edition. Grand Rapids: Zondervan Academic, 2008.

Wilcock, Michael. *The Message of Psalms 73–150.* The Bible Speaks Today. Downers Grove, IL: IVP Academic, 2001.

Willard, Dallas. *The Spirit of the Disciplines: Understanding How God Changes Lives.* Reprint edition. San Francisco: HarperOne, 1999.

SCRIPTURE INDEX